THERE'S SOMETHING WRONG WITH RYAN

A Transparent View into a
Mother's Grief Journey

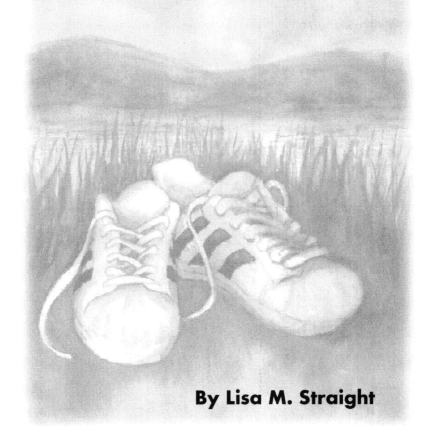

By Lisa M. Straight

There's Something Wrong with Ryan
By Lisa M. Straight
Copyright © 2020

Published by TrueNorth Publishing
10380 Boundary Creek Terrace N., Maple Grove, MN 55369
www.truenorthpublishingdt.com
Manufactured by Snowfall Press, Monument, CO 80132

Cover design and layout: Cheryl Barr
Back cover photograph: Jessica Hegland Photography

All scripture quotes are taken from the New King James Version
(NKJV). Copyright © 1982 by Thomas Nelson, Inc. Used by
permission. All rights reserved.

ISBN: 978-0-9970752-3-6

Published in the United States of America

CONTENTS

Preface

MOST OF US bump along in life dealing with our day to day activities, never believing that the unthinkable could happen. And then it does, wham! It hits you like a semi-truck. *My son is dead at age twenty-two? How can that be? Now what do I do? How do I move on from here?* There would be so many more questions.

I wish I could say believing in Jesus Christ, knowing He loves me and cares for me, made this journey through the dark days of my soul easy. But that was not the case. I was human. I struggled, questioned, and doubted. However, He was with me every day, whether I acknowledged Him or not. You will read examples of how He was there all along, even before this unimaginable test began. He walked along side me, even carried me at times, through the whole journey.

Many other major life changes happened just before I began this grief journey. Jon and I had married just six months before Ryan died. My house was on the market to sell just before and during Ryan's illness. It sold only weeks after his death. One month after Ryan's death, Jon and I moved into our new home. Major restructuring also happened at my workplace as my full-time position changed to temporary part-time status, I suddenly had to supplement that with another job. Within one year I had hit many of life's top stressors.

For twenty years, until I married Jon, my immediate family had consisted of just Ryan and me. I was a single mom taking care of my young child who grew into adulthood. We spent time reading books, watching movies, and roller blading or bike riding together. We became active in our church on Sundays and Wednesdays. Many times, we could be found visiting my parents, Grandma and Grandpa Moe.

My family, as I knew it, was gone when Ryan died. I was the only one left of "us" and did not know how I could survive his loss. I now had a different and new family with my husband, Jon, which God knew I would need in order to survive.

This journey was possible only with God's help, along with the love and support of family and friends. For this I am eternally grateful. His unconditional love and exceeding grace enabled me to say with my whole heart and soul that God is good, even though this terrible trauma happened.

Now I have come to the time in my life to write this book, something that I have never done before or thought I would ever do. I believe God told me that I have a story to tell. He has encouraged me to proceed, even when I needed to set it aside several times. It is with His grace and guidance that I write.

Many of you are family and friends who want to know more of what really happened. Many of the more significant facts were initially known, but questions may remain for you.

Some of you may be struggling with the loss of a loved one as well and are looking for answers. You may wonder if you are alone in feeling the way you do.

Others may know someone dealing with grief. You may wonder what they might be dealing with and what help you could provide.

As I recount my journey of grief and the things that

helped me push through, it is my prayer and hope that this book will bring you hope, healing, and understanding.

"Now may the God of hope fill you with all joy and peace in believing, that you may abound in hope by the power of the Holy Spirit." Romans 15:13 NKJV

Introduction

WHEN I MEET someone for the first time, these are the typical questions. "Where do you live?" or "What do you do for a living?" and then "Do you have any children?" The last question always makes me hesitate. *How do I answer that? Do I say that I **have** or that I **had** a son?*

If I say I have a son, then there will be more questions. "How old is he?" and may continue with "Where does he live?" and "What does he do?" They are expecting the common replies.

I will need to explain that he has died. That wasn't what they expected to hear. They were being social; now it has become a deep and uncomfortable subject. Often the next question is about how he died. I wonder if they really want to know. And if I really want to tell them.

I watch their faces as their minds quickly process this information. Their first reaction is usually sympathy. Next, they might put themselves into my situation. Twenty-two is too young to die. If the person is younger, they may think of themselves and how horrible it would be to die so young or to lose someone they know at that age. Parents may think about their own child or children. They think about how awful it would be to lose them, how they wouldn't want to, or couldn't, go through that.

Sometimes I tell them I don't have children, saying that I only have my adult stepchildren to avoid what usually

4

comes next. Yet, when I do that, I feel as if I have turned my back on Ryan and denied his existence, although it saves both me and my hearer from an uncomfortable conversation.

In these brief conversations there isn't enough time to share or explain much more. Such as all the joy Ryan brought to my life and all I learned by being his mother. I am who I am, in part, by having had him in my life, as well as having him leave this life when he did.

I have had a lot of questions too. I wonder about Ryan's age. He died at 22. Everyone else, his younger cousins and his friends, continue to age. But he will forever remain at 22, at least in our eyes. I wonder what age he is in heaven.

Where is Ryan now? I know without a doubt that he is with our Lord Jesus Christ. He professed Jesus was his Lord and Savior. He had reconfirmed that right before he went into the hospital and while he was there. In 2 Corinthians 5:1 it says, "For we know that if our earthly house, this tent, is destroyed *(we die)*, we have a building from God, a house not made with hands, eternal in the heavens." *But where is that really? Where is heaven?*

What does Ryan do day after day? That question burns in my heart. *Ryan, what are you doing right now?* 1Thessalonians 4:13-14 says, "But I do not want you to be ignorant, brethren, concerning those who have fallen asleep, lest you sorrow as others who have no hope. For if we believe that Jesus died and rose again, even so God will bring with him those who sleep in Jesus." *What is it really like to be on the other side of this life and into our real, eternal life?*

What about God? Where is He in all of this? What about all the questions I have asked Him? My big questions usually begin with "why?" **Why** did you let this happen? **Why** didn't you stop it from happening?

But, the biggest question of all; how do I go on living

without my precious and only son, Ryan? He was a part of me. He was an extension of my life. Everything I did for 20 years was for us.

The life that I knew and my primary role of being a mother, his mother, had radically changed.

My Ryan

BEFORE I SHARE my journey, you need to meet my son Eliason Ryan Cooper. At age eight he decided to go by the name Ryan, with the encouragement of his Aunt Michelle. By junior high and high school his friends often called him Cooper or Coop for short. For clarity, I will address him as Ryan throughout the text.

On July 17, 1980, my son, and my only child, was born. He arrived a month early and his lungs weren't fully developed yet due to Hyaline Membrane Disease. Hours after he was born, they transferred him to Children's Hospital Neonatal Intensive Care Unit (NICU). He would remain there for the first days of his life until his lungs were fully developed. At 7 pounds and 14 ounces he was a big preemie compared to the others. I was in a different hospital down the road. The nurses sent me a Polaroid picture so I could at least see my baby. It sat on my bedside table all the time. I did get a day-pass to go see him once while I was still in the hospital recuperating from having had my baby.

His father and I would go the NICU, scrub up and put on a mask, gloves, and yellow isolation gown in order to enter the unit and spend time with our new son. Staff labeled his bed with Baby Cooper as we had not decided on a name yet. It didn't take us long to know that this son of ours would be named Eliason Ryan Cooper.

After ten days, it was time to bring him home. I wondered if the nurses really knew what they were doing sending this precious child home with me. I was so inexperienced. There are so many things that could happen. I wanted to be a good mother and hoped I would know what to do. In time, with the help of family and friends, I got the hang of taking care of this little one. I enjoyed watching Ryan grow and learn new things.

He was ten months old when his father and I separated and eventually divorced. His father joined the Army as a paratrooper and was stationed in other states; he also went to Desert Storm. His visits with Ryan were infrequent due to travel distances and schedules. We were on our own, and it remained that way until Ryan moved out at the age of twenty. We were a family and he was my life.

We spent a lot of time with Grandma and Grandpa Moe, my parents, as well as Ryan's aunts, uncles, and cousins. Since his father couldn't be there, Grandpa was his father-figure. Their relationship became very close. He had visits with his father's family who loved him, too.

Grandma was always there to love on Ryan. Before he was born, she picked up a chair at a sale to reupholster for his nursery. She said she would be over soon to work on it. I wondered when she would get it done as his due date was getting closer. She ended up working on it after he was born. Every few minutes she would go in and check on him, hold him, or kiss him. I think that was her plan all along.

Grandma and Ryan enjoyed going to the local park to play on their playground equipment. Swimming in her condo pool was also a favorite activity for them. On our frequent visits they would go for walks, play games, watch movies, or read books.

As soon as he caught his first fish, a bullhead at age four during a 4th of July celebration, Ryan became a fisherman. He put the fish into a zip lock baggie so he could show everyone, including strangers, his big catch of the day. His love of fishing continued, and he would fish for hours, even in the rain. Grandpa, who also enjoyed fishing, would grab his poles and take Ryan to the local lakes. These were special times for them.

Nature and being outside were things Ryan loved. Riding his trike, then progressing to a bike and roller blading were favorite activities to bring him to the great outdoors. For indoor fun he enjoyed reading, building with Legos, and playing with GI Joes. When he was nine years old, we had a whole Lego-land built across the floor in the living room. A pirate ship was in one corner, a castle on the other side, and a city in the center. There were cars, trains, and planes as well. We left them there and continued to add to them over the next several days.

Ryan also loved animals and would read a book or magazine about them repeatedly. The first time we took him to the zoo, he was more interested in the sparrows flying around than the monkeys in the cage. Of course, he could see them better as they were down at his stroller eye level. He watched the seals swim for a long time that visit.

A black and white mouse became his pet when he was five. He named it Charley after a mouse called Charley Meadows in a book that he loved. He put a plastic stagecoach from his cowboy set into the cage. Charley would crawl inside and on top of it. Ryan got a kick out of that.

Cats were one of Ryan's favorite pets, and there have been many cats in our extended family. When we moved into our condo, we were able to get our own cats. Soon Tigger and Spook joined our family. He snuggled and played with them. The cats liked to lay on his bed with him. I think he sometimes used that as an excuse to stay in bed just a bit longer.

Around age four, Ryan told me he knew what he was

going to be when he grew up. He was going to be a garbage man so that he could drive a cool truck. But he also was going to be a doctor so he could help people on his route!

Starting at a young age, Ryan's loving spirit was evident as he reached out and comforted others. In daycare, he often helped with the babies, patting their backs to calm them down. This followed through to his teenage years when he helped troubled friends.

Ryan was fun to be with and often led the amusement. People have said his laugh was contagious. Once when he was around five years old, he had us all in birthday hats playing birthday games, and it wasn't even anyone's birthday!

We lived in a condominium when he was about seven years old. Before that we had lived in apartment buildings. None of his friends lived in multiple dwelling buildings. One day he asked me, "If I get a paper route and give you the money I make, can we get a house? You know, the kind that you can go through just one door and then be inside?" I felt terrible I couldn't make that happen for him.

Uncle David Moe, Aunt Michelle Samuelson, and Uncle Mitch Moe were an important part of Ryan's life. He loved spending time with them and their families. From them he learned about being family, how to enjoy life, and many other life lessons. Uncle David often told young Ryan that his dimples were so big that he could eat cereal out of them. Then Ryan would laugh, making his dimples even bigger.

Ryan was the first of six grandsons; no granddaughters were to join them. The next grandson came about five years later. The title *King of the Children* was given to Ryan, as his cousins always wanted to be with him and follow his lead. He usually had a lot of patience with them, even though they were quite a bit younger. He liked to hold and rock the little ones. Many pictures captured him underneath a pile of cousins.

My father's side of the family primarily lived in South Dakota. They began to have family reunions every other year. My father, mother, Ryan, and I would travel together for the eight-hour drive to Huron or Carthage. Ryan looked forward to seeing everyone at these gatherings. When he was nine years old, we decided to make a spontaneous trip to South Dakota, just the two of us. We had a wonderful time with Uncle Bob and Aunt Gladys Moe, Aunt May Fulton, and Aunt Gen Doland. Visiting Uncle Bob's farm was a special treat for Ryan.

On our way home Ryan was upset and began to cry. I asked him what was wrong. He told me he didn't want to leave; he felt like he belonged there. I felt the same way.

The Twin City area is where most of my mother's side of the family lived. Since they were closer in proximity, we were able to see them more often. My mother was very close to her two sisters, Marian Hedlund and Inez Wolfe, so we spent a lot of time with them. They became like second grandmas to Ryan. Many family events, such as picnics and holidays, were held throughout the year. Christmas Eve was one of them.

Every year the Olson aunts, uncles and cousins got together for Christmas Eve. Everyone enjoyed eating and visiting. During the evening, a knock would interrupt the festivities. Who was at the door? Santa! The kids loved seeing him right in the house. He even had a real beard and a round tummy. Years passed before a few chosen ones were let in on the secret of who this Santa really was. My mother worked with this gentleman and made the arrangements for him to make our gathering one of his stops.

Ryan seemed to be missing an active male role model in his life, so I decided to approach the Big Brother organization. It wasn't long before he was matched up with Dan. He liked Dan and they did a lot of different things together. Ryan was self-conscious about letting his friends know about having a Big Brother. He shared this with one of his friends, who responded, "Cool." That was all Ryan needed to hear.

We were blessed with the opportunity for Ryan to attend Northside Christian School from 5th through 8th grade. It was based out of a very active and Spirit-filled church, Church Upon the Rock. He enjoyed their basketball and soccer teams. The 7th grade mission trip to Mexico was a memorable event for him. His heart was touched by the people he met there. He was moved to give one young man his prized Charlotte Hornets basketball cap.

One day, Ryan came home after learning about developmental changes that happen as a young man grows up. He approached me, very seriously, and said, "You might see me bumping into things and knocking things over. Don't worry, it is a normal thing because my body is growing faster that I can keep up with."

I had a hard time keeping a straight face!

He continued, "If I burp or pass gas, I can't help it. If I don't, something inside me might explode."

I laughed with him after that one. Life was never dull with him around. If you were having a bad day, just being around him would lift your spirits.

We began to attend Church Upon the Rock in addition to Ryan attending the associated school. Pastor Gordy Steck, his family, and many other congregational families soon became a very close and dear part of our lives.

They had a phenomenal children's and youth pastor, Jean Lund. She knew how to reach people's hearts, no matter what age they were. Her creativity pulled in those who otherwise may have turned away from the truth of Christ.

Church camp week was a highlight of the year. Ryan was ten years old when he attended the first time. The leaders put much thought and planning into the week's program, and each year a different theme was carried on throughout the week in the Bible teachings, activities and night games. The first day always had an extravagant kick off. Everyone loved it!

Ryan's faith and relationship with Jesus grew, friendships developed, and he had a whole lot of fun! The school and church youth meetings, activities, musical productions, and yearly camps Ryan participated in during his preteens through high school graduation offered him a vast experience many others his age would not have.

As he grew into his teenage years, he dealt with peer pressure. Relationships were important to him. He wanted to fit in, to be liked, and accepted—not unlike most of us. His passion and high energy were a great benefit when bridled in the right direction. But it could also lead to trouble when connected to bad decisions. He struggled through some difficult teenage years. The foundation and relationships that he had from Northside Christian School and Church Upon the Rock were pivotal for him.

Ryan expressed himself creatively through writing. His teachers encouraged him to do more of it. I kept many of his best works. In his teenage years, he often wrote me letters for my birthday or Mother's Day. These were precious and dear to my heart. I am forever grateful that I kept these and did not toss them away. This is one of my favorites he wrote when he was sixteen:

MOTHER,

I DON'T REALLY KNOW WHERE TO BEGING. IT'S
YOUR BIRTHDAY, ANOTHER YEAR OF YOUR LIFE
HAS GONE BY. NOT ONLY THAT BUT I HAVE HAD
ANOTHER YEAR FOR YOU TO BE MY MENTOR, SPIRITUAL
LEADER, AND MOTHER. I AM SO THANKFUL TO GOD
FOR PLACING YOU IN MY LIFE. OVER THE YEARS
YOU HAVE BEEN AN INSPIRATION, AND A SOURCE
OF ENCOURAGEMENT OF HOPE FOR ME. I KNOW AT
TIMES WE DO NOT GET ALONG THE GREATEST, AND I
DON'T ALWAYS AGREE WITH HOW YOU HANDLE THINGS.
BUT I DO KNOW TWO THINGS, THAT YOU DO THOSE
THINGS BECAUSE ITS IN MY BEST INTREST, AND BECAUSE
YOU LOVE ME. THE OTHER THING THAT I KNOW IS
THAT I LOVE YOU. YOU ARE THE GREATEST MOTHER
THAT ANYONE COULD EVER ASK FOR. THANK YOU
FOR BEING THERE FOR ME WHEN I NEEDED
YOU. YOU MEAN THE WORLD TO ME.

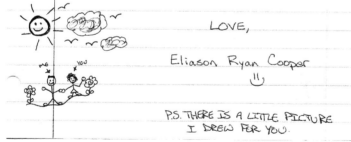

LOVE,

Eliason Ryan Cooper

P.S. THERE IS A LITTLE PICTURE
I DREW FOR YOU.

After Ryan graduated from high school, he did not have a clear direction for his future, yet. He had been working construction jobs for several small companies. Two were with fellow church members who were mentoring some of our young men. Ryan also worked at a local gas station.

He then met his soon to be wife, Lindsay. When they weren't working, they spent time together, getting to know each other and each other's families.

Ryan moved out to his first apartment when he was twenty, just a couple of months before he would marry. He was wed on December 16, 2000. When his wife's baby boy was born the next month in January, he accepted him as his very own. Ryan loved being a father and having a family of his own. It made my mother's heart swell to see him so grown up and happy.

In the summer of 2002, they bought their own home. It was a nice house with a big deck, fenced in yard, and a two-car garage. He also purchased a used fishing boat. He had plans to host fun get-togethers and spend time on the lakes fishing.

Ryan and his family were active members of their church. He even played on the church softball team. He continued to grow in his faith and love of Jesus.

He was in an apprenticeship program to become a sheet metal journeyman. This was going very well for him. The instructors and classmates thought he was a good addition to the class. His father-in-law, to whom he was becoming very close, was a sheet metal journeyman and was mentoring him.

Ryan had made it through his childhood and teenage years. He now had a vision and plan for his future. He was grabbing life by the tail and stepping out into adulthood firmly with both feet.

PART ONE

On Cloud Nine

THE SUMMER of 2002 was a summer unlike any other. I was "On Cloud Nine," "On Top of the World," or whatever other cliché you want to use for a time in your life that is so good, so right, that you feel like you are floating on air.

In 1997, I bought a home for Ryan and me. I had worked hard to renovate much of it, inside and out. I was enjoying the fruits of my labor. My faith was growing, I had a successful career as an RN, my family was doing well. Life was good. Then, as if out of the blue, something happened that made my heart swell; I met Jonathan Earl Straight.

Since Ryan was now on his own, I began to desire to interact with other singles my age. Our church consisted primarily of families with children. I wondered if a larger nearby church would have a single adult Bible study. Emmanuel Christian Center had one I thought I would check out. When I arrived, I did not get out of my car right away. I started to get nervous. I went back and forth in my head. *I should go inside and attend,* and then, *this is not for me, I should leave.* After five minutes of this internal debate, I headed towards the door.

After the joint praise and worship, people went to their perspective classes. A speaker led our group meeting, then we shared in small groups at our tables. Jon happened to be at my table, along with a few others. He listened intently as thoughts were shared by the group. One woman brought up her struggles. When she finished, Jon spent time talking with her. He gave her sound advice and shared pertinent scriptures. It appeared to have been helpful by the peace she had afterwards. I was impressed by his kindness and ability to reach out to her.

Afterwards when we headed out to our cars, he and I started a conversation to get to know each other better. We found out the we both had sons named Ryan, who also shared the same birth year. He had lived in Ladysmith, Wisconsin, as did my mother's family. Our mothers shared the same day and month as their birthdays. It was fun to find out the things we had in common. We kept talking and after a while decided to go across the street and continue our conversation over coffee.

I continued to attend the Bible study until something began at my church that I needed to attend on those nights. A city-wide Koinonia, a single adult fellowship gathering, was held about nine months since I had last seen Jon. I attended with some friends to hear the speaker and have fellowship.

After the message, it was time for food and visiting. I saw a woman who had been at the single adult Bible study class. She said to me, "Jon's here." I thought that was odd, as Jon and I had always engaged with the whole group during those sessions and had not singled each other out. Later, I discovered she had also told Jon a similar thing, "Lisa's here." She saw something between us before we even approached that kind of relationship.

I met up with Jon eventually that night and we had a brief conversation. We exchanged phone numbers and continued to make connections by phone and email. Conversations grew to a desire to be together. Our first time out was for a dinner date, followed by a Christmas Gala. We continued to go to movies, concerts, and dinners.

Each time it became harder to say goodbye.

Jon quickly became my best friend and someone I thought I could spend the rest of my life with. After being single for all but two years of my adult life, I was wary. I did not want my emotions to get ahead of me. I sought God about this. I did not want to be out of His will. When God responded, I believe He all but shook His finger at me and told me that Jon was a gift from Him. All I needed to do was to receive it and open it.

During this time, God was also speaking to Jon in very specific ways about our relationship. Jon had a list of attributes he believed were important to him in a potential wife. He had prayed over it for quite some time, years before we met. The list had been put away when he moved to his current home. Jon found it again, began anointing it with oil, and praying over it. He said it wasn't long afterwards that we met. Later, he said I not only met, but, excelled in those attributes. God had also impressed to Jon that moving forward in our relationship was for my benefit. Little did Jon know how much I was going to need him.

I recommended that we attend my pastor's pre-relational/pre-marital counseling sessions, which I heard were very good and quite detailed. They included several different tests and assignments to identify our compatibility. I felt they would give us the confirmation we were looking for and be a good foundational beginning. Jon agreed and the sessions did give us the confirmation we had hoped for, that we would be compatible with each other. It also brought us together even closer.

Ryan was happy to know that I had found someone to share my time with. He had worried that I might spend my life being alone. He and Jon were able to get to know each other at family meals and activities. They even worked together on a home improvement project replacing my flooring in the dining room. Afterwards, Ryan shared with me that he thought Jon was a good man and approved of him being with me.

Jon proposed to me that May. Of course, I said "Yes!" We had a couple of choices for setting the date. One was in October before the Wisconsin deer hunting season, as many in his family are hunters. The other one was the following May when Jon would be done with the business college degree which he was taking in the evenings after work. He already had an associate degree in Quality Assurance and desired to increase his academia. We settled on October 26, 2002 for our wedding date and were excited to start our new life together.

Shortly after we were engaged, we felt that the Lord gave Jon and me the following verses which would become very special to us.

"For lo, the winter is past, the rain is over and gone. The flowers appear on the earth; the time of singing has come, and the voice of the turtledove is heard in our land." Song of Solomon 2:11 and 12

We both had come out of hard times in our past (the winter) and He was promising a time of happiness (the singing). We were grateful and hopeful for this promise.

Jon said we could have any kind of wedding I desired. It was important to me to share this moment with those who were close to me. We planned a church wedding and reception. The plans fell into place perfectly. I enjoyed making the preparations and all the little details. Jon helped too, but mostly he was just happy for us to spend time together. I couldn't believe this was really happening to me after being single for so long.

October 26 finally arrived. I had a blanket of peace on me. Ryan walked me down the aisle, since my father had passed away in 1997. He was happy for me and proud as we made our way down past the guests, to the front of the church. I was proud of him, too. He looked handsome in his tuxedo, such a grown man. He gave me over to Jon and stepped back to his seat. I did not know there would soon be a deeper significance to this gesture.

During his toast at the reception Ryan said he had thought I might never get married, which made him sad. He said he thought Jon was a "nice guy," then corrected himself and said, "I mean, a really good guy," after which he gave his classic Ryan smile. Jon and Ryan were just getting to know each other, but Ryan already called him and knew him as Dad.

We had a wonderful honeymoon at Bluefin Bay on the North Shore. On the way back we stopped for breakfast. That's when the realization hit me that Jon would be taking me back to my house, but he wouldn't be going back to his house. He would be staying with me forever in what was now *our* home. How wonderful and adventurous!

I had been single for so long, I wondered how things would go as we began our lives together. What issues might arise as we become one? I kept waiting for something to deal with, but nothing arose. It was as if we had always been together. Jon has been my very best friend, confidant, and lover. I have always been able to count on him for anything and trust him with everything.

I am so thankful God brought us together!

There's Something Wrong with Ryan

ON MARCH 16, 2003, Jon and I had driven to Wisconsin to visit his family. On our way back that Sunday we stopped at a church of a pastor Jon knew. A visiting evangelist led the service. At the end of the service, she began to pray for people and shared many prophetic words with them. She saw Jon and me sitting in the congregation and called us forward. She spoke several things over Jon, which he later said only God could have known about. Then, she asked if we were moving soon. We told her we were in process of selling our home and had just put an offer on another house. She said, "Your new house will be a place of peace and healing, but first you will go through a very hard thing." She did not know what the hard thing would be.

It was great to hear her say the house we hoped to be our new home would be a place of peace and healing. But what was the hard thing she spoke of? We were not too excited regarding that aspect of this word. We focused on the good part of the message. As with any prophetic word, we gave it to the Lord and left it in His hands.

We returned home that afternoon and were in the driveway unpacking our car, when our friends from church drove up. It was unusual for them to drop by, especially since we had not been at our church that morning. As we approached their car, we became concerned as we saw the seriousness on their faces.

"There's something wrong with Ryan," they said, and went on to explain. There had been a birthday party after the church service for one of Ryan's friends. Ryan was behaving strangely. They said, "He dropped his drink glass. It slipped right out of his hand and dropped to the floor," and, "He was walking oddly, unbalanced as if he might have been drunk." The message became even more serious, "Something made his face appear different. One side was not the same as the other."

I knew right away that something was very wrong. Was this the hard thing we were to endure? Our friends left, and I called Ryan who was at home by this time. His wife answered and I told her what our friends had shared. She said he had a doctor appointment in the morning. I told her to be sure to keep me posted and ask the doctor about getting a CT scan of his head because the symptoms sounded neurological. I then talked to Ryan, who assured me he was ok and said he was going to get some rest.

For about a month he had been complaining of not feeling well. He was very tired all the time and had tingling in his hands. His wife had been taking him to their family doctor. They ran lab tests and so far, nothing had seemed out of the ordinary.

Next, I called my sister and told her that something was very wrong with Ryan. I felt in my heart that this was not going to be good at all. I fell apart in tears and anguish. I should have gone over that night to see Ryan. But they lived an hour away from us, and I knew he had an appointment in the morning, *right?* He said he was ok and was going to get some rest, *right?*

The truth was I was scared to face my fear, that this might be the worst thing possible. That this could be the beginning of the end for Ryan.

The Day My Life Changed Forever

THE NEXT DAY, Monday March 17, 2003, I went to work on pins and needles while I waited for news from Ryan's appointment. We prayed for Ryan in our morning meeting. I tried to keep busy and get my work done, but my mind was on Ryan. It happened to be St Patrick's Day, and my birthday. However, I was in no mood for celebrating.

Ryan drove his truck to the appointment since he planned on going to work afterwards. His wife followed him in her car. On the way he sideswiped a school bus. He said he was having trouble seeing. I thanked God that there were no kids on the bus, no one was hurt, and there was only minor damage. After the doctor appointment they now planned to have his eyes checked.

The doctor's appointment proved to be futile. They did a quick exam, ran a couple more blood tests and sent him on his way. No CT scan was ordered.

The optometrist, however, was very concerned about Ryan's exam results. He told them that his vision was like someone who had had a stroke. Ryan had a field vision cut. One side of his peripheral vision was closer towards the front of him than to the side. He could see nothing on the affected side unless he turned his head, just as one would need to do in order to see the things behind him. That is why he didn't see the school bus. Ryan was once again sent on his way.

Worry mounted as I waited for news. It was after lunch

when I finally heard the reports of the day. I couldn't believe that these two doctors basically did nothing for him. It didn't seem like he was getting the care he needed. I called Jon to pick me up and we went to see him. By the time we arrived, Ryan was dragging his left leg. It had been a problem that morning, but now it was getting worse. He was so weak and tired. He could barely sit up at the table with us to have a quick bite to eat before he needed to go lie down. I asked his wife what hospital she wanted to take him to. He needed to go. Right now.

We followed them on the hour drive to United Hospital. They had to stop for gas. Ryan got out of the passenger's seat and tried to head for the pump. His wife had to turn him around to go back into the vehicle. Even though he was in such a bad state, he was going to take care of things. My mind whirled. Fear gripped me by the throat. I had a hard time thinking. My heart pounded. I felt sick.

We waited in the Emergency Room waiting room for what seemed like an eternity. I stepped outside to make some dreaded calls, to let people know what was going on, and ask them to pray. Later, I remembered that I had my shamrock earrings on. I took them off and put them in my purse. (I threw them away later since I couldn't stand to look at them.)

The results of the CT scan of his head showed that he had a mass in his brain 6 x 8 centimeters (cms). The ER doctor verbalized disgust and dismay that two other doctors had seen Ryan that day and had not directed him to the hospital.

I broke this news to my mother. Ryan was her first grandchild. I could hardly get the words out. I felt like my heart was being pulled right out of my chest. Tears. And more tears. There would be so many more to come.

He was admitted to the hospital. It was around 1:00 am when Ryan walked into the unit's waiting room to join us.

It was so surreal. It all seemed so dream-like. This couldn't really be happening could it?

After we prayed for him and Lindsay, we said our goodnights and goodbyes. She had prepared to stay at her husband's side that night. Knowing how I was feeling, I can only imagine what was going through her thoughts that night. The rest of us went home. I don't remember what time we got home, but it was very late.

This was the first of many sleepless nights.

Seven Weeks of a Living Nightmare

THE FIRST THING for the doctors to do was to identify the mass in Ryan's brain. A needle biopsy was scheduled for Wednesday. Ryan was placed on many prayer chains and people from around the world prayed. I started to take notes. I needed to keep busy, to do something, anything, and to keep focused as we searched for an answer.

> Tuesday, March 18.
> Ryan is in good spirits, although he is very sleepy. He sleeps on and off during the day, visiting as he can with family and friends in between naps.

> Wednesday, March 19.
> A needle biopsy is scheduled today. First, Ryan must have a "cage" screwed to his head for the computer to give exact directions for the biopsy instruments. This looks like a barbaric torture chamber.

Afterwards, the surgeon came to tell us there were a lot of inflammatory cells that were atypical of a tumor or cancer. They appeared to be more like an infection. Samples were sent to pathology at United Hospital and the

Mayo hospital. We waited anxiously for answers.

Ryan went to therapy for his left-sided weakness. He did not complain of any pain, for which I was very grateful. He did not complain about the situation either; he was cooperative with whatever the staff needed him to do. There was an obvious peace about him. He seemed to have an anointing and grace for such a time as this. Many people noticed and commented on this.

At one point he said aloud, not focused to anyone, "I need to be strong for Grandpa." That seemed like a very strange comment as the Grandpa he was referring to passed away six years before. I wondered why he would say this now. Maybe he knew something we didn't know. *Was he already making the transition to his eternal life?*

Fatigued, he slept on and off throughout the day. He moved from bed to recliner and then back to bed. He couldn't do this on his own anymore. It took another person to help him. This strong young man needed help now to move a short distance. It was hard to believe, and even harder to watch.

With his sense of humor intact, he told a staff member that the nurses kept taking his Snicker bars. He was kidding, as he was the one eating them all. His appetite increased because of the steroids he was receiving for the inflammation. IV antibiotics and anti-fungal medications were also started, even though an infection had not yet been identified.

Monday, March 24.

The biopsy did show many dead or necrotic cells. There is still no diagnosis. A PET scan is ordered for Wednesday. This uses radioactive glucose to show metabolic activity of cells and will show where the active cells are.

Wednesday, March 26.
The PET scan showed active cells around the perimeter of the "lesion" with little to no activity in the center. Ryan's case is baffling the doctors. He begins to spike temperatures up to 103 degrees. A rash is developing on his arms and trunk.

Friday, March 28.
The rash continues. He had been given Dilantin, a drug used for seizure control, as they were unsure if a possible seizure may have caused his accident with the school bus. The Dilantin is discontinued, and he is treated with Benadryl to counteract the adverse effects of the rash.

Physical therapy went well this day. He walked forward, backwards and sideways, both to the left and right. He had trouble moving to the left side because of weakness on that side.

Though getting tired, he also performed well in occupational therapy. He transferred to and from a chair with standby help and was able to walk to the bathroom with the help of one person.

Ryan began to feed himself a little too fast and needed to be reminded to slow down. Some food pocketed in his left cheek, as he had lost some of the feeling there. He was told to check for this as he ate.

Saturday, March 29.
Ryan is spiking temperatures today. He is very weak and having difficulty transferring himself without help. He

cannot walk to the bathroom, so a bedside commode is brought in. He needs two people to help him with this. He also needs someone to help feed him today. What is happening to my son?!?

Another IV antibiotic was started, even though they still did not have an infection identified. Towards suppertime he continued to become even weaker. Another CT scan was ordered, which showed no change. They had him on Decadron to help with the inflammation, which had decreased some, so it looked like he was improving. But now the inflammation had again increased. They still did not know what they were trying to treat.

Sunday, March 30.
Today is a better day than yesterday. Ryan is still weaker, but able to walk to the bathroom with one person helping.

Monday, March 31.
Ryan's right eye is closed shut today due to pressure on the 3rd cranial nerve. He can open it with much effort.

He was weaker again and was using the bedside commode. He appeared to be having difficulty with thought processes when doing something physical, such as transferring from bed or chair. An open biopsy, craniotomy, was scheduled for the next day. This was explained to Ryan, but later when it was mentioned, he asked, "What surgery?" During the day he was able to remember other short-term things, like what he just ate and what month it was, but he couldn't remember being told about the surgery. Perhaps God was protecting him. Later he said he was scared about what was going on with him. This was the only time that he talked like this to me. He had usually appeared at peace and in good spirits, joking around. I'm sure there were many things he was thinking about. I talked with him, tried to comfort him, and for the first time I cried in front of him. True to his nature, he turned his concern towards me and told me not to cry. He then recited Psalm 23, "The Lord is my Shepherd…" Afterwards we prayed.

On Tuesday, April 1, he needed an MRI with computer pads placed on his head in order to have everything in place for his surgery. He was more "out of it" and restless, unable to lie completely still. Due to this, they needed to sedate him for the MRI, which delayed the surgery.

After the surgery the neurosurgeon spoke with us stating he has never seen anything like this. He continued to explain that it was not like a tumor. It was inflammatory tissue with chronic necrosis, dead cells, and tissue. He guessed it might be a viral type of infection or a nonspecific inflammation. He had removed a 5cm square from Ryan's right temporal lobe, mainly to relieve pressure, as well as to get a good sample for the biopsy.

After surgery Ryan went into ICU looking pretty good. He was able to respond with a strong voice. But his left side did not move at all.

Wednesday, April 2.
This is a pretty rough day for Ryan. He has increased swelling around his head from the surgery. He is very quiet, not responding much while I was there.
He is spiking temperatures and his rash continues. He does not move his left arm and has slight movement in left leg.

For the first time he is having pain, post-
surgical pain, and he is given morphine.
He is assessed for eating and
swallowing. He now must have thickened
liquids and pureed food as he would choke
on regular liquids and food.
Ryan is awake for just minutes at a
time; otherwise he sleeps.

The head of infectious disease doctor stated that all the
cultures were negative so far. He said, with despair, he felt
clueless. Samples were sent to the Mayo hospital and he
wondered if Ryan shouldn't be in Rochester at that
hospital, too. He said he would discuss this with the
neurosurgeon.

Soon after, I saw the neurosurgeon in the hallway. He
told me that he, too, was frustrated that they hadn't found
any answers yet. I asked him about transferring Ryan to
Mayo hospital, in the hopes that they might be able to do
something different. He stated without a diagnosis, Mayo
probably wouldn't do anything different but did agree to
send him down and prepared the transfer for Thursday.

Thursday, April 3.
Ryan's face is very swollen on the right
side, his surgical side. His right eye is so
swollen you can barely see his long eye
lashes. His left hand and arm are swollen
from an IV infiltration.
Ryan can respond with one or two words
and is able to raise his right hand up. He
continues to be very lethargic. He continues
to spike temperatures and have the rash.

He was taken to St. Mary's Hospital (Mayo) in Rochester around noon. Ryan waited on a gurney in the hallway for transportation. His Uncle Mitch arrived from South Dakota shortly before his transfer. When Ryan saw him, he smiled and weakly waved.

I went to Rochester and stayed in a hotel to be close to my son. Jon, and other family members, came and went during this time, too. Prayers continued for all of us. Each day I would go back to Ryan's hospital room and wait for an expert to tell us what was wrong with him. And what they were going to do to fix it.

> Friday, April 4.
> Ryan slept well last night. He is in the neuro ICU at St. Mary's in Rochester. His facial swelling has moved down from his face into his jaw and throat. He is responding, but very weak and lethargic. His voice sounds as if his throat is swollen.
> He has a normal temperature. His rash is turning to an "angry" red. The PICC line is removed and cultured, which was negative.

The doctors worked in teams at Mayo. A lot of things were happening now. Ryan had all the following scheduled for one day:
- Speech/swallow test-which was good
- CT/MRI of brain-showing small amounts of bleeding
- Dermatologists exam-full body wraps now for his drug induced rash
- Spinal tap-which was negative, peak inflammation today
- Labs-not infection in appearance
- Lyme's test-negative

- Kidney function tests-ok
- PT eval-stood him up and his head drops/falls as if he were asleep

Saturday, April 5.
    Ryan's temperature is normal. His rash continues. He is very lethargic, barely responding. He does know that he is in a hospital. He didn't want to eat any breakfast. After being so hungry before, this is a change.

Sunday, April 6.
    His temperature is normal, head swelling is better, rash is a little better. He is talking a little better, however is not always making sense, "I saw pancakes go by" and "I have a pair of them in the drawer." He moved his left foot a little, which he hasn't been able to do.

Monday, April 7.
    Ryan ate a fair breakfast today. He did not talk much; it is hard for him to stay awake.

The Occupational Therapist asked him to touch his nose. He was unable to do it until she took his arm and did it for him first.

He thought he had his right contact in and was trying to get it out. Maybe he was getting sensation back and would open his eye soon, it had remained shut since surgery.

Doctors remained baffled. A CT scan showed no

change. The areas affected were the brain stem, mid-pons, thalamus, mid-brain, and basal ganglia. The brain stem area may have been fluid; this area was what was causing Ryan to be so lethargic. Stimulation to this area would not change things. Another drug was started to decrease the disruption at the blood-brain barrier. We were told it would be a wait and see game.

Tuesday, April 8.

Another CT is taken to see if the new drug has made a difference; it has not, so it has been discontinued.

His heart rate has gone down to 38. Given his normal rate is 80, this is a huge dip. He is given medication to counter this. Also, the body wraps are now pre-warmed, and his room is kept warmer with the door closed to keep the heat in to prevent hypothermia.

His albumin is too low (low protein) and a feeding tube is discussed. His wife became very upset so they said a trial of increased supplemental drinks could be tried first. He needs to be fed. He is very weak; rarely responding to us. When he does, it is with a very weak voice. He falls asleep in the middle of breakfast.

There are still no answers. Possibility of another biopsy. CT scan of chest and abdomen are negative.

At one point in the day he visited with me more than he has for a long time, he even winked at me with his swollen eye.

He had a coughing spell and didn't have

enough energy to cough up the phlegm, so needed to be suctioned.

Wednesday, April 9.

Ryan is about the same today. They got him up and put him in a chair for breakfast. He is very lethargic and did not open his eyes while he was fed.

His Uncle David and Aunt Christine came to visit. He always admired David. He mustered up as much alertness as he could, grasped his glasses and tried to put them on, but they didn't fit because of the swelling on the right side of his face. He also tries hard to sit up taller in the bed and opens his right eye to visit.

Thursday, April 10.

It has been one week since he has been at the Mayo hospital.

Today is a good day. He was quite alert for breakfast. His right eye was open, and he talked softly throughout the meal.

I help him with breakfast, holding his head as it wants to fall forward. I tell him he is like the leaning tower of Pisa. Keeping with his sense of humor, he responds "Merci beaucoup" (It doesn't matter that the Tower is in Italy and not France) He is disoriented and tries to eat his napkin and his sheet.

He is scheduled for another MRI. The results showed that the mass effects have improved. Not knowing if the improvement came from the medications or just time, nothing is changed at this point. We are hopeful, this is the first good news we have heard.

Since he is basically stable, he is moved out of the neuro ICU to the neurology floor.

Friday, April 11.

Ryan ate a good breakfast today. His right eye is open much of the time during our visit.

The Occupational Therapist came in to work with him. She asked him to find his left arm. He didn't respond right away, but after about 30 seconds he took his right hand and rubbed his left shoulder.

Saturday, April 12.

Ryan is very difficult to arouse. I helped him with lunch, after much encouragement he did eat well.

Sunday, April 13.

He remains difficult to arouse. Poor intake today.

Monday, April 14.

Ryan remains about the same. The report from the medical team is that they will finish up the two last test slides on Thursday. If they don't find anything, they will be finished. Nothing else they can do. They talk about the need for a feeding tube and a long-term care facility. This is a huge, devastating blow.

Tuesday, April 15.

Ryan remains the same. The Physical Therapist was working with him, and he opened his right eye wide and seemed more alert. She decided to sit him up him on the side of the bed. He held his head up and was looking out the window. (This would be the last time he looks at anything.) It didn't last long, but it was something. Another MRI is taken.

Wednesday, April 16.

Ryan went to surgery at 7am for a tube feeding placement. He is comatose, unable to respond to the world around him. I have lost my son, even though he is still alive.

The MRIs on April 4th and April 15th are compared. There are devastating changes. The inflammatory tissue has increased into the brain stem and now has crossed over to the left hemisphere. Doctors give no answers, and no hope. They feel at a loss and give their condolences.

Saturday, April 19.

Ryan is transferred to a Roseville care center. He is closer to home now and is only a couple blocks away from where I work. He is comatose and being fed through a tube. I stop to see him on my way to work, after work, and whenever else I can. Family and friends visit daily. Prayers continue.

Friday, May 2.
Ryan has been spiking temperatures of 104 degrees. They can get it down to 102 degrees. His feet are ice cold, even with a temperature of 104. He has increased snoring and his respirations have become shallow.

Saturday, May 3.
His temperature remains high and difficult to get down.

Sunday, May 4.
Ryan's temperature remains unstable. His oxygen levels decrease, even with supplemental oxygen. Oh, Ryan, my heart is breaking into pieces!

I spent the morning with him, just Ryan and me. I touched him and tried to hold him while he was lying in bed. I rubbed his short hair. I shared my heart with him, knowing he could hear me, wishing with all I had that he could respond back to me.

But there was just silence.

The Spaghetti Dinner Benefit

AT THE TIME of this nightmare, I was working as the Education Director at a health care facility in Arden Hills. My mother was on her 35th year in the dietary department there. She had been a lead cook for many years, then moved into a supervisor and office role. My first job at age 16 was working with her as a dietary aide. I also had worked there in different capacities as an RN. A core group of employees became a second family to us.

After Ryan was born, we took trips down to the dietary department to visit Grandma and her friends. As he got older, he often talked with the residents on our visits. He always enjoyed being there.

I know it was God's divine plan that I was working there at this crucial time. I was able to work alongside my mother. We were able to take breaks together and see each other daily. Many of my closest co-workers were Christians. Being in a Christian environment made it easy to spend time in prayer, and to know they were also praying for us.

The staff at this facility supported me as things continued with Ryan. The dietary staff, and others, decided to hold a spaghetti dinner benefit on May 6, 2003 to help with the medical costs. Posters went up around the building with Ryan's picture and a description of his circumstance. As I walked up and down the halls, I would glance at the posters and think, *Oh, that poor young man and his poor family. What a horrible thing to be going through.* Then it would hit me. It was my very own son who was on these posters. *No way, it can't be Ryan!* A sick feeling would enter my inner most being.

I was teaching a class on the day of the benefit. It was good for me to have this time committed to my classroom. It would have been harder to have been out on the units of the facility as they prepared for the benefit. Even so, my thoughts were never far from the main event of the day.

Employees attended my class from both my facility and the facility Ryan was in. We still had about an hour to go when one of the employees asked me, "Aren't you the mom of the young man that is in a coma?" And, "Aren't they doing a benefit for him today?"

As you can imagine, it took all I had to answer her. I confirmed her questions, and the other employees gave each other knowing, compassionate looks and then looked at me. My tears flowed readily. All eyes were on me now. I had to muster up all my courage to get through the end of the class. I said aloud, to push me on, "We still need to finish, and we can do this," and smiled weakly. Somehow, I did get through it, being thankful for the overheads and teaching guideline notes.

The facility filled with co-workers, family and friends for the dinner. The classmates and instructor from his Sheet Metal Journeyman course came, too. Even some friends that I hadn't seen for a very long time came to show their support and concern. Approximately four hundred were in attendance.

As I greeted everyone, they all had the same questions, "How is Ryan?" and "What is wrong with him?" There still was no answer for what plagued him. As I looked around the room and saw all those who came to offer their love and support, I was very grateful.

However, I also felt numb and overwhelmed. I had a sense this was like a funeral.

You Should Come

JON AND I returned home from the spaghetti benefit. I was exhausted and numb. A hot bath sounded like it might help bring some relief from the day. I was in the tub when I heard the phone ring. Jon answered it and then hesitantly brought the phone to me. I got out of the tub, wrapped myself in a towel, and he stepped outside the door.

It was Ryan's nurse. She said his temperature was 108 degrees! With his brain stem damage, his temperature regulation was out of control. She told me that I should come. I knew what she was saying. It won't be long, and he will be gone. As a nurse, how many times had I made that call?

After I hung up the phone I stomped on the floor as hard as I could and screamed, "No! No! No! Please don't let this happen!" I didn't want to go because I knew what this meant. My emotions said, *maybe if I don't go, he won't die.* Jon came to my aid. He helped me get ready and we went to the care center. On the way I made calls to others who might want to be there, too.

My family, our pastor and his wife along with another couple from church were the first to arrive. We spent time in prayer with Ryan. Then Ryan's wife and her family came. We watched and waited, taking turns going into his room to spend time with him. I rubbed his fuzzy short hair, touched his face and his hands. These hands had been so strong. Oh, how I wished he could squeeze my hand with his, to let me know he knew I was there. To make one more connection with me.

As Ryan lay there, comatose, laboring for his last few breaths, we waited and watched for the end. *Is this his last one? How can this really be happening?* I called my sister on my cell phone from his bathroom. She was out of town, but I still needed her with me. I was in a near fetal position as I talked with her. I told her it wouldn't be long, and Ryan would be gone. The sound of those words as they left my mouth didn't seem real.

Ryan took his last breath. He moved from life to death. Only one breath separates us from the two worlds of life and death. His body was no longer alive. He was no longer here. He had moved on to his eternal life with his Lord Jesus Christ. No one would have imagined the day of the benefit would be the same day Ryan would leave us.

We consoled one another in disbelief. It was so surreal. I remember looking into my friend's eyes, searching and hoping to find an answer for what had just happened.

Ryan's best friend, Jon Riley, finally made it there. He was upset that he did not make it in time to say goodbye. And, he was angry that his best friend had just left him. Getting off work to come any earlier was not possible. He had wanted to be at the spaghetti benefit but couldn't be there for that either.

We prayed together and then people left. I stayed. How could I leave? My son's body was still there, lying in that bed. I needed to still be able to touch him, smell him, and see him. I didn't want this to be the last time. I didn't want this to be the end.

Finally, it was time to go. Jon Riley was still there, still distraught. I worried about him, so I invited him to come to our house. He came, for which I was grateful, as it helped me to focus on someone else for a while. I was glad to have this time with him. The three of us stayed up and talked until we were ready to call it a night and try to get some sleep.

Sleep? Yeah, right.

Saying Goodbye

THE WEEK after Ryan died was a blur. I still had a hard time believing there was no diagnosis for what led to the death of my son. I was getting phone calls from family and friends whom also wanted to know. These past seven weeks were the longest, and shortest, I have ever known.

Along with her pastor, Ryan's now widow, Lindsay, made most of the memorial arrangements. I was free to spend this time with family. I was numb and moved robotically. My family and I went to Dayton's to find dresses to wear to my son's service. The salesperson made a comment regarding the fun event we must be going to attend. When she found out the reason for our new dresses, she had empathy for us and became extra helpful.

Getting ready to go that day was difficult. I stood in front of the mirror and stared at myself, not believing what was happening. It took extra time to put on my makeup. Jon's daughter, Monica, was there with their new baby girl, Alexis. Even so, it was somber and quiet in the house.

Soon, it was time to go. The trip there seemed to take a long time. We arrived at the church and soon others did, too. There were many beautiful flowers and plants in the sanctuary. People looked at Ryan's pictures and relived memories of him. It wasn't long before it filled up, about 700 people attended. Ryan would have been surprised to see so many there on his behalf.

My brother, David, was in the Bahamas working on a

film project that week. He took a red-eye plane trip back to be there for the service. On his way, he wrote this eulogy to share.

Eliason Ryan Cooper
In the hospital, Ryan told us that he
should be strong for Grandpa Moe.
And strong he was.
And strong he will always be in
character, love, spirit, and faith.
He is loved and in a better place.
I am proud to be his uncle.
This is my poem.
Uncle Davey

big brown eyes,
twinkle with wit and charm,
with friendly dimples and a smile,
that leave us warm.

a smile that lights up a room,
you leave us beaming,
your smile is bright,
let it shine, let it shine,

Shine Ryan Shine
you love people,
big and little,
the Pied Piper to the children,
you're the "King of the Nephews,"

you love life,
your personality is growing,
the sun is always out,
when you're hunting and fishing,

Shine Ryan Shine
Ryan grows before our eyes,

who is this man? I ask,
tall and handsome,
this is my nephew?

you stand tall, young man,
full of pride,
with your family at your side,
and your love for Jesus Christ,

Shine Ryan Shine
Ryan weds Lindsay,
and becomes complete,
he's never been so happy,
you can see it in his feet,

God delivers a miracle,
the pitter-patter of little feet,
it's a boy, it's a grandchild,
it's little Noah,

Shine Ryan Shine
Ryan's sun has never set,
it never will,

He is
Forever young,
Forever bright,
Forever son,
Forever grandson,
Forever husband,
Forever father,
Forever son-in-law,
Forever friend,
Forever classmate,
Forever workmate.

Forever, our beloved Ryan.
Written by David Moe

After the service, most headed to the fellowship hall for refreshments and to spend time together. There seemed to be an unending line of family and friends that wanted to express their sympathies and share a hug with me. I don't know how long this line lasted, but I know I was getting exhausted. I would have liked to talk a bit longer to each one, but it wasn't feasible.

That evening I told Jon's son, Ryan Straight, he was to be my Ryan now. Jon looked at him and told him I meant it. I can imagine he thought those would be big shoes to fill.

Afterwards, many of my family members went to my Aunt Marian Hedlund's to recover from the service. We kicked off our shoes and got comfortable. It was a nice transition rather than going directly home.

At some point I told my nephew, Weston Moe, my brother Mitch's son, that he now had Ryan's role as the oldest cousin. Weston received a pair of Ryan's sunglasses which he proudly wore for a long time. He later had a terrible bicycle accident in which they were damaged. He felt badly about that.

Andrew Theis, my sister Michelle's son, was fourteen years old when his cousin Ryan died. He was very upset and tried to make sense of it all. Andrew, who also has a gift for writing, wrote this poem. He included a graphic of a crown. I was honored to get a framed copy.

King of the Children

ᗯᗯ

Eliason "Ryan" Cooper   Rest in Peace
7/17/1980 to 5/6/2003

> None of us wanted
> Ryan to die... We
> All had to sit down
> And cry....
>
> Now he's free... To
> Be with God for all
> eternity... I hope he
> enjoys his time... So
> high up in the sky...
>   By Andrew Theis

In time, we all headed back to our homes. Each one took with them a flower bouquet or plant from the service. It was a long and exhausting day. But it was also wonderful to receive love and support from family and friends. They made an unbearable day bearable. Witnessing how much they loved Ryan and I was what I needed.

The following day, immediate family members and our pastor met at the mausoleum where his urn would be placed. They have cases, like bookcases, with glass doors. Four of them face each other in a square with room to walk in-between at the corners. In the center is a bench to sit on. My mother and father's remains are in an adjacent case. It is comforting to know they are together, even though that is not where they really are.

Many of the memories from these two days are a fuzzy blur; others are engrained in my memory forever. God provided us with His peace, comfort, and strength to endure. It was a relief to have the formal services behind us.

Now, it was time to begin my work of dealing with grief full steam ahead.

PART
TWO

Ryan's Gone; Now What Do I Do?

The Initial Grief

IT HAS BEEN SAID that the loss of a child is the worst grief to encounter. I was about to experience this personally. Much of grief is hidden from the view of others. It is done in secret, privately, internally. Unless shared, others do not know the extent of the pain and despair one may be going through.

I am describing my pain and suffering during the first two years following Ryan's death in transparent detail. It is my prayer that it will help someone to know that they are not alone in dealing with very hard issues during grief. I also pray that it may help others to look for, or understand, certain signs or behaviors in their family member or friend.

But this isn't the end of the story, praise God! Later, you will read about my journey *through* and beyond the difficult times of grief. Hope endures and remains!

Come with me now as I endure the loss of my precious son during those first two difficult years following his death.

Ryan is gone from my world forever; *now what do I do?* I am left here without my son, without my only child. I am struggling significantly with my identity. My primary identity for almost twenty-three years was being Ryan's mother. *Am I still his mother now that he is gone? How can you say you are a mother when your child is gone?* I do not know who I am anymore.

I feel like there is a huge black hole below me. As if I am dangling above nothingness. Children are supposed to outlive their parents, not the other way around. Children continue the family identity. My family ends here. It is cut off for the rest of eternity. With Ryan, I had the expectation that our family life would continue generation after generation. Now that hope is gone. No one will care about our family memories and experiences, things we held dear.

My heart feels physically ripped apart within my chest. It feels very heavy and painful. I truly have a broken heart. I desperately want to touch him, feel him, and hear him. Everyone has his own scent and a mother knows her child's scent. I miss this, too. I place calls to his cell phone, just to hear his voice on his voice-mail message. I call several times in a row, always wanting to hear more.

Time is now determined by May 6, 2003. It is one day after Ryan died. Now it has been two days. I count the days, weeks and months.

I know that my grief will consume me if I stay at home by myself, without something to occupy my thoughts. So, I go back to work after the first week. Work is a safe place for me. My mother is working here, and I have many friends that check in on me. I do the best I can to keep up with my work, thinking that I am doing a good job. But I am less productive than normal. My supervisor and the administrator are understanding and give me grace.

The daily motions continue. Once I decide to get out of bed, I get up and get dressed. I even put on makeup, which will soon be smeared with tears. These are things I have done every day for years. They are routine and have a semblance of normalcy. I leave the same earrings on for a very long time. It is too much of an effort to decide what I would put on in their place.

I walk through my days in a fog. I try hard to be strong, to have faith. People that know me will expect it, since that is how I usually am, *right?* I put on a happy face, a mask. Then people won't worry about me or ask me if I am ok, *right?* I even try to fool myself into thinking that if I act happy, maybe I can be happy. After all, the saying does go, "Fake it until you make it."

Conversations have become difficult. I try to listen to what others say when they speak to me. But often all that is in my head are spinning thoughts of Ryan, and how utterly wrong all this is. At times, they become like the adults in the *Peanuts* cartoons. I hear their voices but not their words.

I get lost in my grief and in my thoughts. I have moments at my computer when tears flow readily. At times, I don't even bother to wipe them away until I think I am done shedding them. At least for the time being.

Jon knows when the tears will come. He can see my countenance change. I have heard him in the background say to others, "She is going to cry." Tears, so many tears. My eyes are red and the skin around them is raw and painful.

God knows my feelings and is aware of my crying. As a tender-hearted father, He has compassion for me and takes account of these times. Psalm 56:8 says, "You number my wanderings; put my tears into Your bottle; are they not in Your book?"

His comfort comes in through others and the Holy Spirit, as 2 Corinthians 1:4 proclaims, "…who comforts us in all our tribulation, that we may be able to comfort those who are in any trouble, with the comfort with which we ourselves are comforted by God."

Many times, while at work, a friend will stop by, just when I need them. Their comfort comes through a hug and a kind word. A phone call can help pull me out of a puddle of tears.

At home, when I am alone or just with Jon, there are times when a guttural cry comes from deep within. It is a mother's wail and bends me in half. My arms go around my middle with the physical pain of loss. These times are so intense they scare me.

This emotional pain is excruciating. I never understood how young girls could be "*cutters.*" They use a sharp blade to cut into their arms or legs. I understand now why they do it. Their focus turns toward the physical pain, which relieves the emotional pain, at least for the moment. But the emotional pain is only masked and will return. And there would be the addition of the emotional pain and guilt of hurting one's self.

During my intense times of grief, I find myself facing the temptation to cut myself. I have a knife in my bathroom and reach for it a few times. I so desperately want the emotional pain to be relieved. But I never go through with it. I know it is not right. I also sense God's spirit is near me.

The bathtub is a place where I try to relax, try to survive. Here I can be uninterrupted and have time to think, cry, and pray. I have a lot of lavender, which is supposed to help. I have lavender bath salts, lotion, and candles thanks to my sister, Michelle. At times I think about how little it would take to slip down into the water. A couple of big breaths and my pain would be over.

I share my feelings with Jon. He keeps a close eye on me now when I am in the tub. He will knock on the door and ask me how I am doing. At times he will come in and sit in the bathroom to be with me. Sometimes we are silent, other times we talk or pray.

When I drive by myself, I often think about how easy it would be to drive off the road into a tree or a pole. I play it out in my mind. If somehow I survived, when help arrived I would tell the paramedics to leave me alone, to let me die, and refuse their aid.

The struggle with intense emotional pain and the desire for relief plagues me from time to time. But then my thoughts go to my new husband, Jon. I know I can't leave Jon alone or cause him anguish. I can also sense Jesus with His hand on my shoulder to give me peace and strength as the moment passes by. At other times, His Word comes to my mind and tells me how much He loves me. With God's help, I keep my car on the road, keep the knife in the drawer, and get out of the tub safely.

Decision making has become very difficult. Mundane routine tasks are all right; they are attainable. But not tasks that include any decision making. The first time I notice this is in the grocery store. Do you realize how many decisions are made while shoppers go up and down the aisles?

In the cheese aisle, I find myself standing, staring at the different selections. What kind of cheese do I need anyway? I can't think, my head spins and I start to feel panicky. I want to run out of the store. Tears start to well up in my eyes. My breathing becomes fast and shallow. I feel dizzy. I quickly leave the store without getting anything. Jon does the shopping for now. I just can't.

As a nurse, I know these are symptoms of great stress and perhaps PSTD (post-traumatic stress syndrome.) I know what to do to decrease the symptoms, but I am too lost in them to think that way. These panic attacks happen in other situations, too. It is hard for me to be around people. I can't be social right now. Sometimes when I'm at church, with family, or friends, I will tell Jon that we need to leave, often too soon. He does his best to protect me and watch for the signs that have now become familiar.

Sleep becomes difficult and is short lived. I wake during the very early hours of the day. My mind can't shut down. I get up and wander about in the house. Thoughts continually run through my head, most often reliving the nightmare of Ryan's hospitalization and death. I wonder how I am ever going to live with this.

One day I leave work early because it has been an especially emotional day. On a long, empty stretch of road I lose myself in my thoughts. I pass a policeman going the other way. He turns around and puts his lights on to pull me over. He asks me, "Do you know how fast you were going?"

"No, I do not," I replied.

He continued, "You were going 75mph in a 55mph zone. Where are you going?" I briefly explain my situation. He lets me off with a warning. He tells me to slow down as he doesn't want me, or anyone else, to get hurt.

Death and life are frequently in my thoughts. What is the sense of life anyway? Here one day and gone the next. I see a dead raccoon lying on the road. Within one breath he went from life to death. He was alive and breathing, took his last breath, and then he was dead. Ryan was alive and breathing, took his last breath and then he was dead, too.

As each day passes, I reflect that another crappy day in this life is over. I am one day closer to my own death and freedom from this pain. I can see a calendar in my head crossing off the days. I cannot wait until it is time for bed, so I can pull the covers over the day. Even though I know I won't be able to stay in bed long enough.

There are times when I panic, not knowing where Ryan is. I feel an urgent need to find him, to check on him, to make sure he is ok. I often think I see him driving a car or walking in a parking lot. That was him, *wasn't it?* It sure looked like him. My heart beats a little faster. I want to call out to the young man or at least get closer look to check him out. Sometimes I do just that, but when we get face to face, I see that it is not Ryan. My heart sinks, even though I know it is not realistic for it to be Ryan.

I find myself transplanted into another family. I was a single parent of a son. Now I am a member in a family with a husband and his three adult children, with no children of my own. Jon's children have come through their childhood years and were on their own. They did not need a mother, nor did I expect to be their mother, but hoped to become their friend. This new family did not know Ryan very well, nor do they really know me and what I am going through. It feels like an episode on the *Twilight Zone*, where people are moved in space and time to another dimension, away from everything they know.

Just a couple weeks after Ryan's death, my sister, Michelle, graduated with a master's degree in Occupational Therapy at the University of North Dakota. We were all very proud of her. She worked hard to complete this huge accomplishment. Even though she was at the end and finishing her studies, she had packed up her three sons to come when she could to be with us during Ryan's ordeal. I wanted to recognize her accomplishment and hard work. So, we packed up and traveled to North Dakota to celebrate with her.

Here we are, just days away from gathering for Ryan's memorial, together again. But this time for a party. I am proud of Michelle and know Ryan had been, too. But it is difficult for me to pull away from my sadness. I do my best to visit, laugh, and joke with the family. But I am glad when it is time to head home. I have more grieving to do and need to be alone.

People often appear uncomfortable around me. They do not know what to say, so, many times they do not say anything. If someone mentions Ryan, and then I cry, they feel responsible and apologize. But my tears are always just under the surface. It does not take much for them to be shed. I try to assure them that it isn't their fault. But I can see it on their faces that they don't believe me.

That June, Jon suggests going to a local rodeo. I do not feel like going but decide to go. I am hoping we will have a good time, and for distraction from my grief. One of the cowboys looks just like Ryan. I feel my heart beating inside my chest. It is hard to stay in my seat. It takes all I have not to run down to the fence and scream out his name. I know it isn't him, but I can't take my eyes off him. I can't enjoy anything after that. It is not the pleasurable night out we had hoped for.

It seems crazy to me that life can go on all around me, oblivious to my pain. My family and I went to the State Fair on a bus, another attempt to try to get my mind on other things. I notice two young women sitting on the bus, laughing and having a good time. I want to scream at them and tell them, "Don't you know that Ryan just died?"

I am living alone in another world called Grief. It seems like I am in a bubble, separated from everyone else. People can come up to the bubble but cannot enter. I can be surrounded by people, yet I am alone. I can try to enter other people's life and activities, yet I am not fully there. It is like in *Star Trek* when someone has not been completely transported.

This was my initial grief. It ebbed and flowed throughout the first two years after Ryan died. I did my best to get through these dark days of my soul, but I felt like I was just getting by each day.

Towards the end of the second year, the grief pain was less intense and less frequent. Many days would be neutral, not bad, but not good either; this was progress. At other times, I could enjoy being with others or out in the fresh air and sunshine. I continued to have struggles with depression. I did have hope that as time passed things would continue to get better, which was one thing that helped me keep going.

Friends and family offered their love and support which helped me know I was not alone. As I shared my sorrow with others, it would release some of the deep anguish I was holding onto. Reaching out to God through journaling, reading the Bible, and prayer helped me to begin to trust Him more, instead of focusing on why this happened. These were the things that helped me to progress on my journey towards healing.

Words of a Grieving Mother

I HAVE ALWAYS been a sporadic journal writer. Going through this journey of grief proved to be no different. However, journaling would be an important part of my healing. I would like to share some of my writings to demonstrate the progress made through this process.

The following entries were written during the first two years after Ryan's death. These were my cries to God, pouring out my pain and struggles, my heartfelt prayers. Through these, I felt my hope being renewed.

November 24, 2003
Dear Ryan,
You have been the world to me. I love you so much. I love your eyes and your dimples. I love your passion for life and your love for family and friends. You have compassion and have often defended the underdog. You have been tender towards others, many that were much younger or older than yourself.
I am so proud of you, all throughout your life, but especially now all grown up as a husband and father, living in a house of your own. You seem so proud and happy.
I was so excited to have found our next

home in your area. I could just see you stopping by for a quick visit. But you never saw it; you never came.

I'm just so empty now. It seems there isn't anything to look forward to now. How can I ever feel happy again, truly happy, without you to share it with me?

I mostly just want to run away from it all. Everything seems so flat. Everyone misses you so much. You touched so many lives. You felt like you never measured up to others. Well, I wish you knew how much people are thinking that they will have a hard time measuring up to you.

I miss you! I miss you! I miss you! I just want to hold you one more time, to talk to you again. I hated not being able to hear your thoughts and responses once you went into a coma. I was so worried about you. You looked at peace, but were you scared? What would you have said to me?

I'm sorry for falling short. I'm your Mom. I'm supposed to take care of you, protect you. I couldn't take care of you in this. I felt like I was standing on the sideline watching you drown, not being able to save you. We prayed and prayed. I don't understand why God didn't heal you.

I wish I knew for sure that you are ok. I believe that you are, but I want to know what you are doing right now. I want to be with you again.

Thanksgiving is coming up. I know I

have so much to be thankful for, but it is hard when I am hurting so much. How can I be thankful to God when He allowed you to be snatched out of my life? Yet, I'm so thankful that God gave you to me for the time that I had.

I have more questions than answers. It is frustrating and confusing to know that there are no answers that will satisfy me anyway.

I know that you would want me to be happy and live my life the best that I can. Just like you said in the hospital that you needed to be strong for Grandpa; I feel I need to be strong for you. But it is so hard.

I have thoughts of hurting myself, quickening the end. I don't think that I would ever do that. I hope my life here is not long, but just because of that, it probably will be...

My letter ended there, I did not know how to end or sign it. This was the first of several letters to Ryan.

The first big holiday since his death was Thanksgiving. The empty chair was so evident. His laughter that usually filled the room was missing and made a huge void. We had Ryan's picture with a lit candle by it. It made it feel like he was there with us. The next day I wrote:

Friday, November 28, 2003
Lord, you know that it has been hard for me to come to You. I feel like you betrayed me, allowing Ryan to pass away from this

life. I know You have ultimate wisdom and that You love him. I still struggle with trusting You wholly. I want to, but I hesitate. Please forgive me and pour Your grace upon me. Your Word says You are near the broken hearted. Stay near to me Lord, even when I don't receive You with arms opened wide. Help me Lord, I know you already have been. I need Your healing and Your help for me to learn to go on without Ryan. I miss him so. Help my darkness to pass. Help me to spend time with You. Lead me Lord. Make my desert place to bloom.

God knew what I was going through and had compassion for me. He is our good Father and welcomes our questions and our honesty. I knew He would not leave me or forsake me. Psalm 38:18 says, "The Lord is near to those who have a broken heart, and saves such as have a contrite spirit." Yes, my spirit was crushed, but He promised to be near me and to save me from this despair.

After the holidays, I purposed to journal daily, the best I could. I knew there would be much healing for me through this process. I reached out to Jesus, shared my love, as well as my struggles and emotions. As I did, I could feel healing taking place.

January 4, 2004
God, I do not want to lose faith. I want so to trust You wholeheartedly. I prayed and I believed that You loved Ryan and he was in Your hands. I prayed and believed that You do miracles. I do not understand why You did not heal Ryan. Help me believe that You

will heal me from my grief, despair and
depression.

January 6, 2004
    Lord, I feel as though the water is
nearing the top of my head. I am struggling
to stand tiptoe with my nose just out of the
water. I feel the waves come and splash at my
nose, leaving me panicking for air, just to
survive. Yes, I feel as though I am
struggling to survive, but I want to live.
Help me.

January 7, 2004
    I do want to be in Your will. I desire to do
what You desire me to do. But I do not want
to do what is ahead of me, which is learning
to go on without Ryan. How can I??? It seems
so fake, like I'm just going through some
lines in a play. A big facade, that's what
my life is now. Nothing is real. We are all
just players on the big game board of life.
Am I bitter and angry? Yes!

January 8, 2004
    Lord, help my thorn to turn into a flower.
I know You are already showering blessings
upon me. Help me to see them and to realize
that You send them because of how much
You love me. I need more grace, more love,
more power to walk through this valley in
Your righteousness. Help me not to sin in it.

January 9, 2004

Lord, I pray that since I must go through this sorrow and suffering, that You would use it for Your benefit and glory now and in the future. Help me to see past the grief.

January 10, 2004

Lord, thank you for shutting doors that I should not pass through. I am so weak, so tired. I feel like I am aimlessly trudging through this wilderness. Help me not to take the wrong turns.

I could have become angry with God and turned my back and walked away from Him. I could have isolated myself, turned away from my family and friends. I could have hurt myself. But God's grace saw me through this wilderness.

January 11, 2004

Lord, I don't understand why suffering must happen in order to be comforted. But I thank You for those that You have and will put in place for my comfort. I have expressed myself before how I hate going through this "just" so You can use me to comfort others. If it must be, use me to the utmost so it will not be in vain.

January 12, 2004

Help me to trust You wholly, even when I don't understand, even when I feel so wounded and alone. Help me to understand that You will see me through victoriously. I need to know that You love me. I still feel that somehow, I must have done something wrong and I'm being punished.

January 13, 2004
People tell me that I'll be stronger when this is more behind me. I don't feel like I will ever be strong again. I feel like I'm in a never-ending wrestling match of my mind. I'm so tired of thinking. When can I just shut it down?

When people said things like this, it seemed to contradict my thinking at the time. I would have a hard time to believe or receive it, even if it was true. I usually would listen, smile weakly, and thank them. Perhaps seeds were being sown?

January 14, 2004
God, You are in my tomorrows. How do I learn to live without Ryan? How do I move on to tomorrow knowing he will not be there?

January 16, 2004
Today on my way home from work I felt like I got a word from You. I do not fight against flesh and blood, but against powers and principalities. And the battle isn't even mine, it's Yours, even though it rages in my own mind. For the first time since Ryan died, I feel Your peace. I feel separated from my anxieties. I can't fight this battle any longer. I want and need Your peace.

February 12, 2004

The air above me seems dark, not always black, sometimes just grey. I long for the day when peace will totally rest upon me and the joy of my salvation returns. I know You are my God and my heavenly Father, who knows all and knows best. But that doesn't take away my hurt or emptiness, or my thoughts of my future life on earth without Ryan. Lead me to peace.

February 15, 2004

Today was a big breakthrough day! During praise and worship at church I told the Lord that I loved Him, not just words from my head because that's what I should do, but from the depth of my heart, and I really meant it. This was the first time I could do this since Ryan died. Then a woman, who was new to our church, got up and went to the front of the church. She felt God was leading her to share a verse with us. It was Song of Solomon 8:6-7 "Set me as a seal upon your heart, as a seal upon your arm; for love is as strong as death, jealousy as cruel as the grave. Its flames are flames of fire, a most vehement flame. Many waters cannot quench love, nor can the floods drown it. If a man would give for love all the wealth of his house, it would be utterly despised." Wow! That spoke so clearly to me that You heard me and received my love and that You have not ever stopped loving me! I got up and shared this with the church. Afterwards, Pastor said when he heard that verse this morning, he had thought it was just for me. I want to love You more and more. I know You have not stopped loving me. I can never thank you enough. The best I can do is to just love You and serve You.

February 19, 2004

Today I had to go into the facility where Ryan had his last days for a work function. It is the first time I have been there since Ryan was there. Has it really been nine months? Memories popped in and out of my head like commercials interrupting a drama. I was glad to get done and leave. Tomorrow I go to see a psychiatrist. I wonder what she will say. I just don't want to do this! I don't want to live without Ryan! I just want to scream at the top of my voice. NO! But what good would that do? It won't change anything.

February 20, 2004

Today I went to see a psychiatrist. It has almost been a year since Ryan went into the hospital. I am struggling with symptoms of depression and am concerned about how I will react to these first anniversaries coming up. She asked many good questions. But one question rang in my head all day long, "Do you have any guns in the house?"

Jon does have guns. I had not given them

any thought. They were put away, but not locked. I told Jon about what she asked. He said he had thought about them the week before. He quickly got locks in place. Lord, protect me from thoughts of hurting myself. I have tried a couple different anti-depressants throughout the year but had side effects from them. Another anti-depressant is prescribed; hoping it is helpful as I head through these next few months reliving Ryan's illness and death a year later.

February 23, 2004

Today I feel more alive than I have for almost a year. I know God is working in me. Also, the new medication I'm on must be helping. Whatever it is-thank you Lord. I can't accept all this as an opportunity, but I know I need to move forward into God's will for my life here on earth. Only by His grace and compassion will I be able to do it.

I have had the privilege in the past of going to Florida several times with my mother and aunts for a spring get-away. This year we decided to go again, not to vacation, but to choose a new environment instead for a time of healing. Here are some thoughts I had during that time.

March 1-5, 2004

Here I am in Florida with Mom, Aunt Marian, and Aunt Inez. It has been a wonderful mind break—just relaxing on the beach, listening to the waves, watching the birds and people go by. This morning as others sleep, I want to take time to write. As I watch people walking on the beach, I think that person will die someday—so will that one. Their place will be vacant. Life and death. Death is so final. Here one second, gone the next.

I still don't understand why Ryan had to leave so soon. What I would give to have him back for just a moment. Is he really doing okay now? That is the hope I hold onto, that he is finally enjoying the greatest peace and joy imaginable.

But my empty heart still aches. He was my child, my only child. I don't want to just bide my time going through this life wondering who is going to die next.

On Mother's Day the year after he died, I wanted to go somewhere special. Ryan loved fishing, so I wanted to be by a waterfront. Jon took me to a state park. After we walked awhile, he left me alone and went on a walk. He stayed within a short distance so he could keep an eye on me. Here are my thoughts that day. This becomes another good-bye letter, resonating the things I loved most about Ryan.

May 9, 2004

Mother's Day. Where do I begin? How do I go about this? I need to say goodbye, but, how can I?

Jon and I came to William O'Brien State Park on the St. Croix River today. It is a beautiful spring day. There is a slight breeze and the birds are busy singing. You would have enjoyed this, Ryan. You would have had your fishing pole out. Today is Mother's Day but my reason for celebrating it is gone. Ryan, you are not here. You are not here with your big, brown eyes and big smile. You had become such a strong, confident man. I am so proud of you.

I tried my best to teach you things, support you, encourage you. You took what I gave you, what you learned through church and school, friends and family, and then made it your own.

People say that I am still a Mom. I don't see that right now, not without you here, present in this world. My heart just aches for you. I miss your voice, listening to you share such grown-up things as a husband and a father. You were respected both by peers and those above your age and status.

I want to hold you so badly, just to touch you and smell you one more time. How can I go on living when you are dead? I can barely write that word. My mind cannot comprehend it. Yet, you are dead (here is that word again!) no longer living in this world. I can't call you to find out how you are doing. I must believe that you are okay, I must have faith in what I can't touch, see or hear.

Yet, I must go on living. For you, for Jon, for God. I don't want to be wandering in this wilderness until I die, too. Lord, help me to live as you will for me to live. I cannot do it in my own strength. Your Word says when we are weak, You are strong. Well, I have never felt weaker in my life, so I've never needed Your strength more than now.

Ryan, I wish you could hear me, know what I'm saying, and how I feel. I believe that you did know how much I loved you and always will. I will never forget you. Besides God, you were my life. You were the reason for so much that I did.

But I must say goodbye. Goodbye to you in this life. Goodbye to seeing you grow up. To becoming the best sheet metal journeyman anyone could have wanted. Goodbye to you having your children, to you and Jon knowing each other even better. You two so quickly became friends as well as family. You even called him "Dad" and really meant it.

I say goodbye to visits at your home. You were so proud, and rightly so, of your home and family. Look at what you accomplished by the age of twenty-two. I couldn't wait to spend time there with you.

I say goodbye to the way you were with children, so patient and loving.

I say goodbye to you at our family gatherings. There will always be an empty place from now on. The energy and lighthearted spirit you brought into the room will be no more. All the Christmas celebrations to come won't be shared with you. As I shop and see something that would be perfect for you, it will stay on the shelf. Your birthday will come and go, and yet you will not get any older. Others will age; your cousins will age and even be twenty-two and older someday. Those times will be hard for me.

We have the Moe reunion this year. You were at the last one, with your new family, so proud. You were all grown up, the next generation, and now you are gone.

I don't think I will ever stop noticing the empty places. Imagining what it might be like if you were still here.

The only thing that helps me get through, make some sort of sense of it all, is that your leaving so soon kept you from enduring some very hard things and that God loves you and was merciful by allowing this to happen.

So, I will begin this year, going into the second year of your passing, saying goodbye. I know it will be an ongoing process, but I do need to say goodbye. To admit that you have really died. You quit breathing; your heart stopped. You left your earthly body. It was cremated, burned to ashes, and put in a box. How could that happen if you did not die? It is not you in that box; you are not there.

Eliason Ryan Cooper, born 7-17-1980, died 5-6-2003. Ryan, your body died but you will always live in my heart. There's plenty of room for both you and Jesus. You will live in memories and stories, as well as family and friends.

Lord, You say that this lifetime is but a fraction of eternity, but it seems so long. It feels like it will be a very long time until I'm with Ryan again.

Ryan, today on Mother's Day I say goodbye. I love you with all my heart and always will.

Love, Mom

In January 2005, one year and eight months after Ryan's death, I wrote in my journal that I was so tired of feeling like I was walking in mud, and that it was keeping me from moving forward. I went on to say that I didn't want to be such a weak and doubting person. I knew moving forward with God would give me the strength to go on.

My relationship with God continued to get better, but it needed further improvement. I still couldn't say He was a good God and really mean it from my heart. My journaling continued.

May 17, 2005

Thank you, Lord, for today. Help me to be "in tune" with you so that you can use me. Plug me in! I don't want to be disconnected anymore!

(And after reading Psalm 28) My heart does trust in Him and He does help me. My heart does leap for joy and I will give thanks to Him in song.

May 27, 2005 (after reading Psalm 32)
Lord, I want your unfailing love to
surround me. Your Word says it surrounds
the man who trusts you. Help me put all my
trust in You again. I need to trust You. I
need to have your love surround me!

My journal entries vacillated between doubt and pain, and faith and hope. My faith was present, even if it sounded feeble. Jesus tells us that we do not need a certain measure of faith to be effective. Matthew 17:20 says, "...for assuredly, I say to you, if you have faith as a mustard seed, you will say to this mountain, 'Move from here to there,' and it will move; and nothing will be impossible for you."

I was reaching out to Jesus, but my grief and despair were barriers to receiving the help that I needed. However, after those tough first two years, I did begin to break through and was on my way to healing.

Jon Riley, My Other Son

RYAN AND I have had a select few people, besides family members, who have been an important part of our lives. They also have been a sanctuary of love and hope for me after Ryan died. This is one of them.

I have another who is like a son to me, Jon Riley. I believe it was God's divine purpose to have Jon in our lives before Ryan became ill. He continues to be a blessing and a support to me. Many times, I received a call from him right when I needed a lift.

Jon and Ryan met during youth group at our church. They soon became very close, closer than brothers. Whenever they could, they spent time together. They even had the same job on the night shift. Jon would stay with us so they could ride together and then sleep at our house after their shift.

Ryan had wanted to get a tattoo in high school. I told him if he really wanted one, he could get one after he turned eighteen-years-old. For his eighteenth birthday, he and Jon went to get the tattoos that they created. They had them placed on their upper arms. Ryan's was a cross with a crown of thorns, Christ's blood dripped from the cross. Jon had a large, ornate cross. They wore their new tattoos proudly.

When Ryan was married, Jon naturally was his best man. He was proud to be there to support his best friend on the big occasion.

When Ryan became ill, Jon was distraught, of course. He visited him at the hospital as much as he could. He was in the National Guard and ready to be deployed, as our country had just invaded Iraq. The war played constantly on the TVs in the hospital waiting rooms.

Jon's visits were almost as meaningful to me as they were to Ryan. The love he had for Ryan and their special friendship will always be there in Jon's heart. It has continued in a relationship between Jon and me.

Losing his best friend had been devastating to Jon. He wanted to do something special. So, he added to his tattoo Ryan's full name, Eliason Ryan Cooper, across the top, his date of birth on the left, and his date of death on the right.

He also bought a couple of Labrador dogs shortly after Ryan died. One of them he named Cooper, which was what Ryan's friends called him. Cooper became his close four-legged friend with whom he could share his sadness unconditionally. When his dog became ill and was put to sleep, Jon suffered another big loss. He didn't realize why losing his dog was so difficult for him until his brother pointed out that it was like losing Ryan again.

Jon wrote several poems, one of which he shared at a gathering we had six months after Ryan died. They were written so well and right from his heart. I am blessed to have copies of these and am touched when I read them. The gift of writing was another thing that Ryan and Jon had in common. Here is one of Jon's poems.

WISHING

Crashing and thrashing the thoughts begin to pound like waves in the ocean. My head pounds wondering what I can do but I watch helplessly as you die. Wondering why God let this happen, I begin to question my own life.

Wishing it was me and not you I begin to cry
wondering why God chose you instead of me. My dream
is to spend time with you as we used to.

I remember that smile and the way you lit up
the room, always the life of the party and everyone's
friend. Although anyone comes after you better
watch out cause you're coming for them.

Wishing it was me and not you I begin to cry
wondering why God chose you instead of me. My dream
is to spend time with you as we used to.

Time passes by and I begin to deal with what I
need to. I miss you so much but know that I won't
see you again until the day I die. I know that you are
in a better place right now and looking down on me.
I hope that you are smiling and that I make you
proud.

Wishing it was me and not you I begin to cry
wondering why God chose you instead of me. My dream
is to spend time with you as we used to.

By Jonathan Riley

I know Jon felt abandoned by his best friend. He
wanted to share his life events with Ryan such as getting
married, having his daughters, and buying his first home.
It is rare to have such a close friendship today, especially
for young men. To have it ripped away so soon has been
difficult for Jon.

Mother's Day came the week after Ryan died. Jon
stopped by with a Mother's Day card for me. What a
wonderful surprise! Every year I endure the loss of Ryan
during the week of Mother's Day. But Jon continues to
remember me on Mother's Day, my birthday, and on other
holidays. He checks in on me and keeps in touch with a
call, a card, or on social media. What a huge blessing he
has been to me!

This relationship reminds me of when Jesus, on the
cross, looked down on his mother and said to his disciple

John, "Behold, your mother." Jon has stepped in to take Ryan's place at these times, so I won't be without a son.

I feel that, in a way, Ryan lives on through Jon. When you are close to someone, your life is shaped by them. As I watch Jon with his family and friends, I can imagine Ryan right there with him, too, having fun, supporting him, even being sad or angry with him. When Jon hugs me, I feel like I'm not only getting a wonderful hug from Jon, but also one from Ryan.

Our Friend, Dave Herrick

DURING RYAN'S ordeal, a very special friend, Dave Herrick, and his family, became part of my journey. He began to struggle with cancer at about the same time Ryan began his health decline. They had been a part of our lives for years, but little did we know how entwined we would become that spring of 2003.

Ryan and I spent several years attending one of our church's weekly fellowship groups at Dave and Georgia Herrick's home. They had three children close to Ryan's age. Dave became a wonderful male role model for Ryan. We spent time with them at family camps and other church functions as well.

Dave and his family helped this single mom raise her son, as they offered support and encouragement during times of struggle. They also were part of shaping Ryan into the man he was to become. They were like family to us.

It was difficult for our small church to have two beloved members dealing with grave situations at the same time. Prayer sessions were held for both Dave and Ryan. Dave said he was praying for Ryan as well. I'm sure Ryan would have been praying for him, too, if he could have.

Dave came to Ryan's memorial service. He sat in the back row with his family. I didn't see him until we were leaving the sanctuary. Our eyes met, speaking volumes. I kept walking out into the foyer as others walked behind me.

I had hoped to see Dave at the gathering in the fellowship hall afterward, but he did not have the physical ability to attend. If I had known that, I would have run over to him as I left the service. I regret not being able to greet him, thank him for coming, and tell him how much he meant to Ryan.

Just four days afterwards, Dave went home to Jesus, exactly one week after Ryan did. His funeral, too, was exactly one week after Ryan's memorial service. It is a comfort to know they are together.

Dave's daughter, Rachel, had sung at Jon and my wedding just months before Ryan and Dave had their last struggle in this life. Little did we know the connection we would soon share.

Dave's wife Georgia and daughter Jami and I attended a grief support course a few months after Dave and Ryan's deaths. Those were very special times sharing intimate grief topics with friends who were going through their own grief journeys at the same time.

Why God, Why?

ON A ROLLER COASTER of my thoughts and emotions, I felt like my world had been turned upside down. I had so many questions and felt so confused. *Why was Ryan's life cut short? Why did he have to die just when he was doing so well and was so happy? Did he do something wrong?*

The Bible says if one honors their mother and father, he will have a long life. I thought that Ryan honored his parents the best he could, but he did not have a long life. This promise seemed hollow.

I had believed that I could trust God with anything and everything. I had trusted Him with my son, Ryan. I knew He could have stopped his death, prevented it. I had cried out to Him to heal my son. *Didn't He hear my cries?* Prayers from around the world were lifted to Him on Ryan's behalf, yet he was not healed.

What was it that took Ryan anyway? The doctors were never able to give it a name. *What reason do I give for Ryan's death?* It was not cancer or an infection. It was not an accident or an injury. There is no name that I can blame for my son's death. I believe it was an act of Satan who hates those who love God. Not having a definite reason identified has been difficult for me.

God loves me, right? Then, why would He allow this to happen? This did not feel like love to me. I believed that He had given Jon and me the promise that, "...the time of the singing had come…" Song of Solomon 2:12. *Then, why did this happen now? Was the singing done so soon?*

God is good; that is what the Bible says, "…No one is good but One, that is, God." Mark 10:18. *How could a good God allow a mother to go through this?* This didn't seem good to me. *How could a good God cut a young man's life so short?* This didn't seem good for Ryan.

I worked so hard to be the best mom I could be. *What did I do wrong? What should I have done differently?* I didn't understand why God wanted me to go through this.

Eventually, I was led to a verse that I believed in my spirit was the reason God allowed this to happen. Isaiah 57:1-2, "The righteous perishes, and no man takes it to heart; merciful men are taken away, while no one considers that the righteous is taken away from evil. He shall enter into peace; they shall rest in their beds, each one walking in his uprightness." I believe in my heart of hearts that Ryan was saved from something more terrible.

I kept trying to go to God with my pain and questions, *"Father, I am raw with grief, tormented in my thoughts and emotions."* But I wondered if I could trust Him with that. I felt betrayed. *Will He say I have little faith?*

I believe Jesus is my Savior. But I was not sure if He was Lord of all of me if He permitted this grief. No, I couldn't trust Him with this.

"God are you there?" "Lord…?" He must have been there, but He was making me figure this out on my own. Didn't He care what this was doing to me?

"God I…" I was confused, not sure what I believed about God anymore. Maybe I was foolish to believe before. *What reason did I have to believe now?*

"I'll just read the Bible." That led me to wrestle with all my feelings about Him and what the Bible said. The more I read, the more I felt the contrast between His promises and my pain. My grief was not a lie; maybe His promises were a lie. *Was I being punished?* Wait! *Was that the enemy causing*

this confusion?

We continued to attend Church Upon the Rock for several years after Ryan's death. It was my church family and a safe place to be during my pain. I wanted to be in the presence of my friends. Even though I struggled with my thoughts toward God, I wanted to be in His presence. I often cried on and off throughout the service. I so desperately wanted to find His peace, hope, and joy again.

Many of Ryan's friends were there. He had attended youth group and camp with them. He grew into adulthood with them. I would look at them and wonder why Ryan wasn't there, too. It did not make sense to me. This was another obvious reminder that Ryan was gone.

I still worshiped God and said I loved Him, which I did. I knew this was the right thing to do, but it was from my head more than my heart. I could not say that He was a *good* God at this time. Those words could not come out of my mouth. Many of the praise and worship songs spoke of His goodness. I couldn't sing those songs—not yet, anyway.

One of the songs that helped me, even though it was hard to sing, was *Blessed be the Name of the Lord* by Tree 63. I usually couldn't sing more than just a few words of the song, and I did it through my tears. "On the road marked with suffering; Though there's pain in the offering; Blessed be Your name…"

One verse that has been a rock for me throughout this journey has been Romans 15:13, "Now may the God of hope fill you with all joy and peace in believing, that you may abound in hope by the power of the Holy Spirit." His joy comes from deep within. When I think of happiness, I think of a fleeting emotion that is dependent on circumstances. No, I was not happy about the situation I found myself in losing Ryan. However, I did still have His joy!

These tug of war conflicts would continue for several

years. I would find the peace and answers I needed when I would seek God through prayer and the Bible. At other times, I felt like the heavens were closed to me when I tried to figure things out on my own. That is when I struggled with despair and discouragement. I would allow my emotions to take priority and keep me in a cloud of grief.

As my journey progressed, I learned that I needed to move on from asking the *why* questions and begin to *trust* God again. I Corinthians 14:33 says, "For God is not the author of confusion but of peace..." As I began to trust God more, I did begin to regain a sense of peace and hope.

Our New Home

GOD WAS PRESENT in my life and was making provisions for my journey as Ryan's illness began. The process of buying Jon and my new home would prove to be an important part of this. Looking back at how all the pieces came together so perfectly, I see nothing short of a miracle.

As Jon and I began our life together, we planned to find a house north of the Twin Cities. Ideally, it would be one with a small acreage and a waterfront. We kept looking at houses on the internet and in person. None of them seemed right for one reason or another. Then, one day Jon and I were looking on an internet site and saw what seemed to be the right place. As soon as I saw it, I felt it was not just a house, but our home. It also happened to be close to Ryan's new home. We made an appointment for a viewing and could not wait to see it.

When Jon walked in, he said he felt goose bumps. He said he had never experienced that before. We both felt right at home. We made an offer on March 5th that was contingent on selling our house. We were so excited to hear that the sellers had accepted it. Now all we had to do was sell our house, pack, and move.

Shortly afterwards, Ryan went into the hospital and his ordeal began. The last thing I wanted to do then was think about selling our house and moving. Things were hard enough. But we had set things in motion, so kept moving forward with the plans.

The housing market was good at the time. We felt our house was priced right, even a little low, so it should sell quickly. We had approximately fifty showings, but no offers. Not even a low one! It seemed strange. Our realtor could not understand why no offers were presented.

On May 21st we were told that the owners of the new home we wanted had another offer that did not have a contingency. We had one day to decide what we were going to do. Would we let this house go and forget about moving for the time being? Or would we take the contingency off of our offer, having faith that our house would sell soon, but taking the risk of having two mortgage payments until it did sell?

I was not in a very good frame of mind to make decisions. I could not understand why this was happening. Considering the current real estate market, things should have gone smoothly and according to plan. We prayed and thought about it. It did not seem right to let the house go. On Monday, May 22nd we had the realtor take the contingency off of our offer. That same day a couple looked at our house and placed a very good offer on the table, with no contingencies!

We closed on the sale of our new home on May 31st, just three weeks after Ryan died. We moved that weekend with the help of family and friends. Since we did not close on the sale of our old house until June 25th, we had extra time to finish the move and wrap things up there. This took a lot of stress off of us. As we reflect, we can see how God had orchestrated everything to work out best for us.

Our realtor told us the previous owners of our new home had lost a baby boy to sudden infant death syndrome. One of the reasons they moved was to leave the location of their nightmare. Though a place of anguish for them, it was to be a place of healing for us. We felt it was more than a coincidence that both of us had had a son pass away.

Having to take care of the moving details plus work at my job was exhausting, but it also kept my mind busy. All the support and help from friends and family made the details possible. Friends and family came to help me pack. As we packed, we talked, cried, and prayed. These were special healing times for me.

On moving day, friends from church and family came to our aid. Even some of Jon's family came from Wisconsin to help. It was to be a new beginning. I now had a new family, a new home and a new life.

However, it was a new life that could not include more than memories of Ryan.

A New Course for My Life

AS I LOOK back over the past sixteen-years, I can see that dealing with my grief has been a process. Has it really been sixteen years since Ryan died? This process has not been a linear one that goes straight from point A to point B, and then on to point C, but a progression that has gone forward and backward, and up and down. It has been like the tide coming in and going out. The tide doesn't just show up. It is a definite process and it takes time. The waves come in and go out, the tide progressing a little more with each one. Eventually the tide completely comes in.

The shoreline is uncovered as the tide recedes. It reveals that the tide brought with it not only water, but sand, driftwood and other miscellaneous items before returning to the sea. Each wave brings change, carrying in some of the water's hidden items to be left behind. Other things are washed back to sea, not to be revealed, at least for the time being. Perhaps with the next tide . . .

That is how my journey has been. Moving forward, then going backward. Different issues or struggles brought up at different times to be discovered or revealed. I believe it must be done this way since we could not handle everything all at once. We need to identify and work through a multitude of issues as we move toward healing, and we need to do it at a pace that we can handle.

When a child dies, we miss them, their physical presence, from that day forward. But that is not the only loss we face. Their death produces a domino effect of many other losses and issues. These include other relationships, as well as social and life events, that cannot be the same or may not even take place.

Holidays are reminders that Ryan is no longer with us. There is an empty spot in the space where he should be. They are no longer the joyous events that I used to look forward to, like his birthday, but in time I have adjusted.

Time is now determined differently. My time is now forever referenced from May 6, 2003, when Ryan died, and my world was permanently changed. The first year I counted the days, weeks, months. After that I counted the years. Each time an anniversary date arrives, I have a hard time believing that so much time has passed since that fatal day.

There appears to be three legs to my journey. The first two years after Ryan's death were, of course, the hardest to go through. Those were the initial raw stages of grief.

Years three to five, the second leg, found me beginning to heal from the open wounds of the loss. I began to trust God again. I also began to learn how to live without Ryan.

The fifth year to the present is the third leg of my journey. Intermittent times of depression and grief remain, but, year after year, these became less frequent and less intense. God's hope and peace increases within me as I walk and talk with Him and put more of my trust in Him again.

Leg One

These first two years were tough years. They were the dark days of my soul. There is a reason they call this the *work* of grief. Going through the initial grief was excruciating and exhausting. This leg of my journey had more rugged mountains and hills than peaceful valleys. However, the level of intensity and frequency slowly diminished as I worked through anguish, confusion, and sleepless nights.

It was critical for me to work on finding my new identity. My life now had two very distinct parts. One with Ryan and one without him. My husband, Jon, and his family were my family now. I had to redefine who I was— at least in my perspective.

I wanted someone to tell me what to do. To take me by the hand and walk me through this process, step by step. I desired to know what to expect and what life was going to be like moving forward. What did I need to do to find the peace and contentment I had had before Ryan died?

Reading, for pleasure and learning, is something that I like to do. This led me to look for books about others who had lost children. I thought a *Grief for Dummies* how-to-book would have come in handy. I found several books about losing babies and young children, but I needed something that related to the loss of a young adult. One about losing a child whom you raised and helped to move forward into adulthood. I had looked forward to enjoying the next stage of being a parent. That joy was ripped away from me. I wanted to know how others coped with that type of loss.

I found books on grief, both Christian and secular. It was helpful to know that I was not alone in experiencing loss. My reading also confirmed there are no real answers to all of my questions. Some answers I looked for did not exist. Just as every loss is different, every journey through grief is, too.

My family, immediate and extended, is very close. They have always been there for me. As a single parent, I could not have done all that I did, including getting through nursing school, without them.

I received and greatly appreciated the love and support they poured out throughout this tragedy. I could not have done this without them either. They have made me feel very safe and loved.

I also have friends who have been very supportive and helpful throughout the years. They included Ryan and me in their lives as family. They continued being part of the hedge of love and protection that surrounded me now.

Family and friends were able to keep me going, when I did not think I could. I had to choose not to isolate myself. It would have been easy to stay home in my sorrow, but that would not have been helpful to my healing.

My husband, Jon, offered a different kind of support. I was a newlywed as I went through Ryan's ordeal and began my journey of grief. This isn't the way most newlyweds start their lives together, but God knew that I was going to need Jon to make it through the hard times. In fact, I believe that being married to Jon saved my life.

He provided the safety and security I needed. Being with Jon, I enjoyed moments of freedom from heartache and pain. These were much needed reprieves. I know they were gifts from God that gave me strength to carry on.

Even though Jon had been acquainted with Ryan for a short time, he also grieved his loss. However, it was not as all-consuming, which enabled him to comfort and support me as he did.

Our first anniversary was five months after Ryan died. We went up north to the same place we had had our honeymoon. I wasn't sure how I would be emotionally during the trip and had mixed feelings about going. It ended up being a wonderful time. It was as if God put a shield around me from intense grief and pain. For two days I experienced a reprieve and enjoyed our time away. It was another wonderful gift from God for both Jon and me.

During those difficult first months, I thought I should reach out for help in other ways, too. First, I tried a support group for parents of children who had died. At the group Jon and I attended, there was a sense of hopelessness. As parents shared how they were doing in their struggle with grief and loss, many seemed to be stuck. Some had been attending for many years but still felt an intense level of hurt and devastation. Of course, this was all new to me. I had no idea how long my own struggle would last. I sensed an overall feeling of oppression there and did not find this group helpful.

Next, I attended a support program called *Grief Share*. I was blessed to attend this with Dave Herrick's wife, Georgia, and one of his daughters, Jami. It was Biblically based with weekly videos of credible people sharing real-life situations. Some were well-known pastors, Christian speakers, and authors. They did not gloss over their darkest moments. They conveyed hope as they shared how they walked through grief with God's help and His Word.

Each week, after the video, we got into small groups to share our thoughts and feelings regarding the topic for the night. We ended with prayer and fellowship. Our workbooks included daily devotions and homework to focus on throughout the week. I found that this course offered the support and hope I needed, even though it seemed to only touch the surface at the time. I have later gone back and reviewed the assignments again, getting more out of them each time. This continued to aid my healing.

I went to a psychiatrist who prescribed several different antidepressants. Due to side effects I experienced, it was difficult to find the right one. Eventually, I did not take any. I am not sure how much help they had been. Then I saw a Christian psychologist. Could he really understand my struggles? How could he? This was a personal journey that I had to go through on my own. I was glad to talk to someone that I did not know. He did give me good suggestions regarding my depression and grief struggles.

I attended a class on depression at church. Depression is multifaceted and it takes courage to face and overcome, many times with the support of others. I learned new things that I could apply to my situation. It was also comforting to know that I was not alone.

Initially, I chose not to talk to God about my true feelings as I thought He might judge me. I tried to hide my unbelief and distrust from Him. He knew all about me and what I was going through but continued to love me anyway. He didn't change. My circumstances changed. He remains the same, "Jesus Christ is the same yesterday, today and forever." Hebrews 13:8.

Re-establishing my side of my relationship with God was a process. As my emotional mountain diminished, I was able to draw closer to Him again. I believe my initial pain and emotional distress were barriers that prevented me from receiving His help, which I so desperately needed. In hindsight, I wish I had been more brutally open and honest with Him from the very beginning.

I also had a difficult time reading my Bible. It was exactly what I needed, but it was hard to receive from it when I was having ambivalent feelings about God. In time, I was able to spend more time in His Word and receive His love and comfort. When I did read scripture, I was drawn to the Psalms. It was there that I found examples of imperfect humans being loved unconditionally by our Lord. I found the much-needed grace, encouragement, and hope that I looked for.

The Psalmist David struggled with his emotions, and

had times when he questioned God, too. He shared with God the dark days of his soul. I found comfort that a "man after God's own heart" like David had also understood many of the same issues I was dealing with.

This Psalm described exactly how I felt.

> "I am weary with my groaning; all night I make my bed swim; I drench my couch with tears. My eye wastes away because of grief…"
> Psalm 6:6 and 7

David also questioned God's lack of attention towards him and wondered why he had to go through his suffering.

> "I will say to my God my Rock, 'Why have You forgotten me? Why do I go mourning because of the oppression of the enemy?'" Psalm 42: 9

He questioned his own emotions and why he felt depressed, even when he knew God was the answer to lifting his state of mind.

> "Why are you cast down, O my soul? And why are you disquieted within me? Hope in God; for I shall yet praise Him, the help of my countenance and my God." Psalm 43:5

However, David was able to resolve these issues with God's help. He found the peace and hope he searched for. These Psalms encouraged me greatly. Hope and peace returned when I embraced them.

We held an event at our church which we called *Remembering Ryan*, six months after Ryan died. Friends and family gathered to share their hearts and memories about him. We had a box for handwritten memories. A video camera captured the spoken thoughts and memories.

Several of his friends got up to share and said Ryan was their *best* friend. Afterwards, Pastor Gordy said, "Ryan had more best friends than anyone else I know." Another shared when in a room full of people, Ryan made you feel like you were the only one there, or the most important one in the room. Also, he would probably be one of the first ones to greet us in heaven. His friends commented that Ryan knew his future and goals, many of which had already begun to happen. "I don't even know what I am going to do tomorrow!" said one of Ryan's friends.

My brother, David, created a memorable DVD compiling pictures of Ryan's life. He set it to music that was meaningful to Ryan. This was a highlight of the evening.

With the passage of time since his death and being in a more relaxed atmosphere than at Ryan's memorial service, people were more able to share their hearts. They also connected with each other in their own grief journeys. I believe this was a healing event to all who attended. I am glad we arranged it.

On June 5, 2005 Ian Andrews, who has a large healing ministry, spoke at our church. At the end of the service he had us pray for one another. I felt a tingling, warm sensation from the back of my neck up to the top of my head. I believe God was healing me of the depression I had struggled with since Ryan passed away. (I would need to continue to trust God in this to walk it out.)

At church that evening, we had a Eucharist communion, a focus on being thankful. I shared that I was thankful God kept me safe these past couple of years and that He was lifting my depression. A friend shared a couple of scriptures with me, the same ones God had impressed upon me earlier. They spoke of placing my feet in large, open spaces and freedom! (Ps 31:8)

During an evening session at church on June 7, 2005, just over two years after Ryan's death, I sensed a very real touch from the Lord. I felt as though something was literally physically lifted. I believed that the remaining depression that I had been under was completely removed. Later that evening, a friend spoke this verse over me, "I would have lost heart, unless I had believed that I would see the goodness of the Lord in the land of the living. Wait on the Lord; be of good courage, and He shall strengthen your heart…" Psalm 27:13-14

The words "land of the living" resonated in my spirit. I knew that God, and Ryan, wanted me to be in the land of the living, not the dead. I needed to shift my focus from Ryan's death to the life that surrounded me, even to the life that Ryan had now. This was imperative, although I still had times of doubting God's goodness.

Yet, to make that shift, I felt like I would leave Ryan behind, turn my back on him, and abandon him. His death was the last physical connection I had to him. If I let that go, I would no longer have an earthly connection to him. I panicked just thinking about it.

Mourning had become a familiar place—one I was hesitant to leave. Stockholm syndrome is a strange phenomenon in which over time a captive identifies with the captor and won't leave, even if there is opportunity. I understood part of this now.

Yet, I knew it was time to move forward and that if I didn't, I would be stuck here for good. Later that evening I wrote this:

> June 7, 2005
>
> I feel like I just woke up from a two-year coma. It is good, but weird. Suddenly two years are gone. I feel very vulnerable, like a new fawn learning to walk. Things will never be the same; they can't be. I need to learn my new dance, my dance without Ryan, so gingerly I take my first few steps.

In order to find hope and peace, I needed to reconnect with God and be able to receive from Him. I also needed to say goodbye, a real goodbye, to Ryan and move back into the land of the living. Choosing to release my grief allowed me to move forward in my healing journey.

I survived the first terribly hard two years, but I did not do it alone. I had the much-needed love and support of my family and friends. And it was also due to God's great unconditional love, His grace, and mercy, along with His protection. As I read the Bible and spent time in prayer, I was being renewed.

Leg Two

At the end of the second year of Ryan's passing, I felt more release of depression and mourning. I purposefully chose to start to let go of my grief and to reconnect with God. These were important steps in my healing process.

The years 2005 to 2008 marked the second leg of my grief journey. As the intense cloud of mourning lifted, I experienced things differently. I still went through stages of grief again but with changes. My eyes were opened wider with more knowledge and awareness. It was as if God was moving me forward, lovingly kicking me out of my grief nest to teach me to fly.

Although the intense grief lessened, I continued to struggle to find my way. I still felt different from everyone else with a feeling of separation that I couldn't shake. I continued to seek my new identity but felt like I didn't belong anywhere.

My journal entries in the early part of this leg spoke of ongoing struggles, but with more hope and determination to overcome. The Psalms continued to give life to my soul.

June 25, 2005.

Psalm 39 speaks of a man wrestling with God about his sorrows and questions. He felt like a stranger with God.

Psalm 40: 1-3 tells of what the Lord does for us. "I waited patiently for the Lord; and He inclined to me, and heard my cry. He also brought me up out of a horrible pit, out of miry clay. And set my feet upon a rock, and established my steps. He has put a new song in my mouth- praise to our God; many will see it and fear, and will trust in the Lord."

I feel a vast number of troubles is surrounding me. BUT so are Your blessings! Every blessing you pour out, I will turn it back to You in praise!

July 8, 2005

Psalm 42:11 "...Hope in God; for I shall yet praise Him, the help of my countenance and my God."

My healing stretched forward, only at times to be pulled back again, as if I were connected to a bungee cord. I felt the enemy saying, "Where's your faith? How come you can't move forward in this?" Yet, I did put my hope in God, and I did praise Him, because He was my savior and my God! Guess what, it saved me from the pit of mourning! *Where would I be without Him??? I don't even want to know.*

July 19, 2005

Sunday was Ryan's birthday. He would

have been 25 years old. It's so hard to believe that he's "stuck" at 22 years old. He was such a wonderful son!

Psalm 43:2-5 "...Why do I go mourning because of the oppression of the enemy? Oh, send out Your light and Your truth! Let them lead me; let them bring me to Your holy hill and to Your tabernacle. Then I will go to the altar of God, to God my exceeding joy; And on the harp I will praise You, Oh God, my God....Hope in God..."

Lord, You have sent forth Your light and truth! Thank you!!! I do love you! Let Your light lead me to Your presence, may Your truth lead me to knowing You more deeply. Within Your light no darkness can stay-it MUST leave! So, I say, fill me, my life, my days with Your light so that the darkness that wants to consume me, surround me, just cannot be!

Your truth and KNOWING it will set me free. The truth is that You ARE a GOOD God, You ARE full of GOODNESS! Your truth is that whoever believes shall LIVE! Ryan lives with You forever. The truth is that this time on earth is but a fleeting moment. The truth is that You love me and died for me.

Lord, help me to see Your truth, not the lies of the enemy. You are full of lovingkindness. When you bring me to Your dwelling place, Your mountain, then I will go to the altar of the Lord. I will lay down my life, my dreams, my Ryan before You (with Your help). I will put my hope in God, and I will praise Him!!!

July 31, 2005
This week I told Jon that I felt like something new was birthing inside of me and it wouldn't be long before it was born. I just felt like something was going to change soon.

At church today, a friend shared a word with us. He said that Jon and I, with God, would be birthing something. (Yes, he used that same terminology just as I had been thinking earlier) That it would be us with God—not on our own and that God's part is the hard part-the heavy burden, and ours is to take the light yoke. (Could that be in reference to writing this book?)

Lord, I don't know what this is all about, but I give it to You. Show us the way.

We celebrated our third wedding anniversary on October 26, 2005 by watching our wedding video. It was good to revisit such a blessed event. Pastor Gordy's message was on covenants, to each other and to God. It was a good message then, and it had even a deeper meaning after losing Ryan. It was, however, difficult to watch the parts with Ryan in them. He was so handsome, and such a sweetheart!

On December 14, 2005 I had a heart-to-heart with God. I brought my extra-large baggage and placed it before Him.

Lord, I'm so glad You don't look at me and say, "Now what!?!"

Here I am again wondering how I can keep so distant from You. I don't like it, but I am afraid to change, to let go of this season, it seems so final. I am hanging onto the threads of what I feel are left of Ryan.

So here I am not understanding and not really knowing what to do. You know all about me, so please help me to be honest with You, for me. I'm taking a bold step and want to change because I am not really living now. I know You have better plans for me, and Ryan wouldn't want me to be like this either.

So, I am going to open my heart to You. Take the crust off and make it a heart of flesh again. Forgive me and have mercy on me. I feel like such a failure, but I know that's not the truth. Forgive me for my unbelief and for pushing You aside. I can't do this without You. I invite you into my pain, into my suffering. Forgive me for putting up a wall between us. I want it down! I break it down right now! I give You freedom to come in any time. Help me if I hold You back again. Come, come into my wilderness. Walk beside me, talk to me. I want to listen. I want to hear Your voice. Nothing else matters but you.

I invite you into my innermost painful areas, even those I am not aware of. Help me to heal and move on from this painful

valley. I need to know that You still love me.
That You're not too disappointed in me.
 Forgive me for being a "people-pleaser",
even towards You. How can You stand us???
I/we must just tire You out!
 I forgive You for taking Ryan home.
Your ways are not my ways. With Your help
I will move from not understanding to
accepting and trusting You.
 I open the ugly parts of my heart to You.
Tell me anything I need to know, to move
away from, and to get rid of. Your Word
says that You restore my soul. Boy do I need
it restored! Come Lord Jesus!

I began to feel pulled away or disengaged from my church. I did not like this and thought it was just me in my depression. So, I tried my best to ignore it and push it aside.

But I believe that it was God getting me ready to move on to another church. I needed to move forward but found it difficult when I was surrounded by so many memories and shadows of Ryan everywhere at my present church. Some of the very best years of my life were at this church. I loved the pastor and the families here. They meant so much to me. It would be difficult to leave.

I eventually talked to Jon about it and we began to look for another church to call home, even though I did not want to. No other church would ever be the same.

We met with Pastor Gordy and his wife Jana to tell them this bad news. He recommended a church that had connections with our church over the years. We checked it out and felt that it was very similar to our church. It was Holy Spirit led, and the congregation was like one big family, very friendly and welcoming. We ended up joining and spent several years there. I missed everyone at Church Upon the Rock but knew this was where God wanted us—at least for the time being.

During this time, we were invited to join friends on a trip of a lifetime to Hawaii! The week of tropical fun in the sun with them was terrific. Snorkeling the beautiful reefs and watching the colorful fish was great. Protected sea turtles even swam alongside of us. We attended a delicious and entertaining luau as well. It was a wonderful time.

Yet, even in beautiful Hawaii, I continued to feel some grief cloud over me. Thoughts of Ryan were not far away. However, I was beginning to find myself experiencing more times of happiness.

I began to learn how to live without Ryan. It was a time of discovering who I was now, and that I really could survive and live without him. I would try to focus on Ryan for who he was, and not on those last seven weeks of his life. The battle of depression and dealing with my loss of Ryan subsided greatly but had not been completely removed.

I continued to press into God and into His love.

Leg Three

As the second leg of my journey came to an end, I found myself more released from my world of grief and able to participate more fully in the life around me. My new identity was taking shape and I began to accept my new roles.

In 2008, the beginning of the fifth year without Ryan, I continued to work on accepting what had happened. Time does not heal all wounds, but it does help to minimize the intensity and frequency of the pain as we learn to live with our loss. At this time, God began to do a new thing in me. I felt a new stirring within my spirit.

Finally, I was able to say that God was good again and really mean it! This may not sound like such a big deal, but it was huge to me. This had been a barrier to wholeness, and now it was broken. Yea!

I began to accept my new role as a mother who had lost her son. Not to accept it, nor to move forward, would have been a waste of my life, which is a gift from God. It would have been a negative mark on Ryan's legacy. He had lived life to the fullest, reaching out to others, enjoying family and friends. He would not have wanted me to stay in grief for the rest of my life.

One evening about seven months after Ryan's death, I became agitated with my thoughts towards God. I had been a victim of domestic abuse in the past. God had brought me through that, and throughout the years has used me to comfort other women who had also suffered abuse. I complained to Jon, "If God took Ryan away from me, just so I can comfort someone else, well, I don't want to do it!"

That very next day we received a phone call that a teenager, the son of friends from church, had died very unexpectedly. I believe God was preparing me the night before to be able to help meet this very need.

The teen's mother had been a faithful friend who had gone to pray for Ryan during his last days. She had caught me in the hallway one day and commented about me being so strong and that she could never go through something like that. She didn't realize that I wasn't as strong as she thought, that I was a mess inside. Who would have thought she would have to survive the pain of losing her son, too?

My heart broke for her, and it brought Ryan's death crashing back in on me. I asked God how I could help someone else when I was so engulfed in my own grief. Of course, I did reach out to her and was glad to do so, even if I felt totally inept. She and I were able to talk and get together a few times. We also have been able to keep in touch through social media. We have sarcastically said that we are in an exclusive club that no one else wants to join, *Mothers Who have Lost their Sons.*

God continues to cross my path with parents, mostly mothers, who have lost sons. Most of the young men had died in their early twenties from a variety of ways including murders. I have listened to their stories and pain. I have cried and prayed with them.

As the ten-year anniversary of Ryan's death approached, I could not believe that he had been gone for double digit years now. That felt so terribly long! It felt important to do something with family and friends in honor of Ryan. Not a memorial service, but a time of fellowship and fun, something he would have loved to do. I invited his friends and their families, my friends and my family to be together again, to have outside fun and share stories about Ryan.

People came and found their spots on patios and other sitting areas. Some enjoyed the outside games. After eating, we formed a circle and shared stories and memories about Ryan. Each one blessed me deeply. It was a nice day, and many people came to show their love and support, for which I am grateful.

Social events became more pleasurable and less stressful. However, holidays continue to be difficult, especially Christmas. The Christmas season was one of my favorite times of the year. I love the joy and giving spirit, all the decorations, and the gatherings of family and friends. The family traditions that Ryan and I developed over twenty years are gone. The celebrations we have can feel empty, even though I am with other family members whom I love and enjoy.

My mother died two years ago so the traditions we had with her are gone now, too. My siblings and I are creating our own now, and I am still trying to find peace with these new traditions.

My new family has been changing, also. Jon's family has grown through marriages and grandchildren. His son, Ryan, was married in August 2008. His family includes his wonderful wife, Mary, and their daughter, Madison.

Jon's daughter, Monica, was married to Bryan Prince in September 2013. He has been a blessed addition. They each had children before they met and then had two together. Their family includes seven children all combined; Alexis, Kaiden, Gabriel, Malakai, Liddiah, Jonathon, and Ashleigh. Each one is precious and loved!

Joshua, Jon's middle child, goes to church and lunch with us on Sundays. He also spends some weekends with us and enjoys family visits.

I have become part of this growing family. New traditions are finding their place. I love this family and cherish our times together.

The anniversaries of Ryan's birth and death continue to be sad and sometimes tough. I like to go to a lake or park on those days, since Ryan loved to be outside. It gives me time to get away from everything else to think about Ryan. I will smile, cry, or laugh as I reflect on his life.

In God's timing, we returned to Church Upon the Rock. It is great to be back with our pastor and church family. It has been like going home. As I enter this next season of life, it is good to be with those with whom I have shared so many of life's ups and downs.

Just as any journey starts with a first step and is followed by another step and another, so my journey has been. This journey that started like a roller coaster with abrupt twists and turns, ups and downs, has mellowed into more of a boat ride with an occasional small squall here and there. I still think about Ryan often. I know his spirit is alive and he is lives in our hearts and memories.

I try to focus on the good things in life and on the future. I am forever changed and there are ways that I am different, but that is part of life. We never do stay the same as time goes on. As I have moved forward from grief, I have tried to use it for my benefit, as well as for the benefit of others, which makes me a victor and not a victim. There are many popular sayings regarding this such as, "What doesn't kill you will make you stronger," and, "Will you let this make you bitter or better?"

God's hand has been on me for this journey even before Ryan became ill. He blessed me with Ryan and our close relationship. My family, both extended sides, are full of love and compassion. Words cannot express my gratitude for them. God planted me in a church with a wonderful pastor and supportive friends. Ryan's good friend Jon Riley has been like a second son to me and means the world to me. During tough times God knew I would need my husband, Jon, to support me and He brought us together. I am not alone because He has blessed me with a new family.

As time has progressed, I am able to be more grateful— grateful for the time I had with Ryan, grateful for God's unconditional love for Ryan, and grateful for God's unconditional love for me. It is evident that God has been with me and did, in fact, answer my prayers within the journey itself.

I have noticed that I do not handle stress as well as before all this happened. I sometimes become overwhelmed more easily. Mild panic symptoms may appear, but these are usually brief and rare.

Knowing this, I try to be kind to myself. I watch for times when I am getting overwhelmed. I pray for God's peace that is beyond our understanding, and for His grace to see me through. I try to watch my schedule and not over-extend myself. At times, I need to decline requests from others and hope they understand.

Today I am finding a new normal. I can truly say that my life is a good one, although a grief scar does remain. I still have times of sadness and missing Ryan, but they do not consume me as they did before.

My journey has not come to an end. It never will. Having Ryan die at age 22 is something I will never get over. He will forever live in my heart and I will always love him dearly. I continue to learn how to live with this loss here, in this life, along with discovering I can still have an abundant life here and now. I am thankful that he has just stepped into eternity before me and I will share precious fellowship with him again.

PART THREE

My Suggestions for Your Grief Journey

I DO NOT propose to be a grief expert, but having experienced deep grief, I know what was and was not helpful in my journey. I believe in sharing with others, just as others have shared their experiences with me.

William Baillie Hosfied, MD University of Minnesota, Department of Psychiatry stated through personal communication with Wayne D. Samuelson, PhD, Family Psychologist, that severe, painful grief lasts one year for every year of the relationship with the deceased. But with help, the intensity and frequency will diminish.

The three things that helped me the most were; my relationship with Jesus, being with kind, compassionate family and friends, and finally, taking care of myself the best I could. At times, that meant asking for help when I needed it.

Remember, no two grief journeys are the same. Healing tasks will be different as well. I am praying for you as you continue your own grief journey.

- If you do not know Jesus Christ as your Savior and Lord, you can change that right now! Just talk to Him. Here is an example prayer. "Dear Lord Jesus, I know I am a sinner, and I ask for Your forgiveness. I believe You died for my sins and rose from the dead. I trust and follow You as my Lord and Savior. Guide my life and help me to do Your will. In Jesus. Name, Amen."

- Pray and get real with God. Tell Him all the messy, ugly things that you are dealing with. He already knows what is going on with you anyway. Nothing surprises Him.
- Put God's Word in you, even if it is just one verse. There are so many options today. You can read the Bible, listen to it, or watch it on a TV, laptop, or your phone. You could ask someone to read with you if that would be helpful; most would be happy to do so. His Word has comfort and hope, and that is what you need right now. If it is too hard right now, give yourself the grace to be ok with that, too. Like the *Footprints in the Sand* poem, He may need to carry you for a while.
- Know what truth is versus the lies. The truth is that you had someone awesome in your life. The truth is that they died. The truth is that you are alive and are going to move forward through this. The lies focus on your loss, on things that you could have done better, that your life will never be good, and that God has something against you or your loved one. We can't live perfect lives. We do the best we can at any given time. The truth is, God thinks the world of you! He made you and loves you!
- Let your emotions out, but do not let them rule you. You may need to pull up your bootstraps and put on a happy face for certain circumstances. But don't stuff things where they will not get dealt with. Share these emotions with someone you trust to be non-judgmental.

- Be kind to yourself. There is much you are going through emotionally, physically, and spiritually. You will need all the strength you can get. Eat right, sleep well, and exercise. Get outside and breathe in the fresh air. Just being outside with living plants, birds, animals, and different scenery can help change your focus, at least for the time being. I joined an exercise class and kept my gear in the car in order to stop there right after work. I knew if I went home first, I probably wouldn't get to it.
- Keep a regular routine. Knowing what will happen day after day will reduce the stress of needing to plan or having to make decisions.
- Perhaps, this is a good time to start fresh and make a new routine, if it doesn't add stress. Start with something easy for you. However, do not change too many things at once.
- Do not start complicated new projects or make big decisions. Postpone them if you can. You need your energy for grieving, and sometimes to just get through the day, week, and month.
- Do not have high expectations of yourself. Do things in small steps. Take care of the bare necessities. Prioritize them, make a list and cross items off as you complete them. This may give you a sense of control and accomplishment, which is something that you may need right now. If something is more than you can handle, pass it off to someone else or ask for help or leave it for another time.
- Struggling with an identity change? No one can take away who you were with your loved one. That is a relationship that is real. They live on in your heart and memories. You are who you are, in part, because of them. Find and focus on the

113

purpose in the primary roles that you have now.

- Social difficulties. Go slow but engage with your closest family members and friends. Be sure to take time for yourself, but don't isolate yourself either. Even if it is hard, being around others can be healing. You may find it better to be in a larger group, so you aren't as noticeable. Or perhaps for you, a smaller, more intimate group of those that know you best would be a benefit.
- Preoccupation with death may consume you. It is hard to enjoy anything when death is always on your mind. Death is a natural part of life, just as being born is, but with loss and grief it may be hard to think like that. Focus on your loved one's life. Think about your life with them and the wonderful times you shared. Call someone to talk about special dates or anniversaries that are coming up in the future. That may help your focus to shift away from such thoughts.
- Find a purposeful task that can help you to re-live memories constructively. I reorganized my photo albums and made books with only Ryan's pictures. I enjoy picking up the books and looking at the different seasons of his life.
- Go somewhere your loved one enjoyed. When you are there, think of them sitting with you. What would you say to them now? You could take pictures, do a video journal, or write down your thoughts.
- Dealing with self-destructive behaviors? Do not keep them a secret. Share them with someone you trust and allow them to intervene. Don't worry about what that person will think of you;

you need to set your pride aside. If you didn't share and something happened, they would be devastated. Avoid being alone for prolonged periods of time. Those are the times your mind can get into very deep, dark, negative thoughts. The loved one you are grieving would not want harm to come to you because of their loss.

- Do not compare your grieving to others in grief. Everyone is different and their grief will be different, too. There is no set timeframe for grief and mourning. Give yourself as much time as you need to grieve. Don't rush it. It will take the amount of time that it takes.

Grief and Other People

OUR SOCIETY does not do a very good job of handling grief. Three days of funeral leave and back to work you go, ready or not. How long should the grieving process be? When should one get over it? Should it be the same for every person and every loss? The truth of the matter is, it is not something that you ever really get over, but instead you will learn to live with it for the rest of your life.

Many people supported me while Ryan was in the hospital and immediately after his death. However, most of the support and contacts soon faded away, except for my family and a few friends.

I believe there are many reasons for this. Initially, people are drawn to tragedies. People slow down to see traffic accidents or watch tragic news for hours on end. They can't believe it has happened or is happening. It is a natural human desire to provide care and concern for others. This nature to help is driven both by our emotions and by the adrenaline involved with the situation. But once the initial tragedy has ended, people tend to continue on with their own lives and routines again, as they should. Although I would have welcomed more contacts, I understand.

After hearing about Ryan, many people, mostly mothers, told me that they could never go through something like that. I would see their face change, becoming very serious and concerned, even horrified at times. That usually ended the conversation.

People may become fearful and wonder about something similar happening to them. They might put themselves in that place but believe that they would never be able to cope. Or they may have survivor's guilt, feeling guilty that they are grateful the loss did not happen to them. That can make them put distance between themselves and the situation since it is too hard to think about or face.

People can also be uncomfortable with another's pain. If talking about a loss brings tears, it looks like pain, and the moment can become uncomfortable. Yet tears are healing. Stuffing the pain and tears can be a setback to a healthy grieving process. It is also important to understand that just because someone doesn't cry, it doesn't mean they are not grieving. Everyone has a unique process for handling grief.

I wanted to remember and talk about Ryan. I wanted others to call him by name and talk about him. I wanted to know if, and how, this loss was affecting them. Were they grieving, too? It meant a lot to me to know Ryan's loss affected others, that he had been a good part of their lives and that they missed him, too. But most of the time the concern was focused on me, and out of respect they did not share about their own mourning for Ryan.

I needed people to ask me how I was really doing, to dig deeper than the socially expected, "How are you doing?" I needed them to listen, really listen, to what I was saying. Of course, this kind of conversation takes time and the right setting, so typically it seldom happened.

Often people would respond to hearing my son had died by telling me they knew what I was going through. They would then proceed to share their own experience about someone else. This made me feel like what I had just shared did not matter. That Ryan did not matter. It was very hard for me to switch my mind from Ryan and my grief to listen to their story about someone I did not know. I did not want to hear their stories. It took too much energy to try to focus on what they were telling me. This was never helpful for me. I often cringed inside as soon as they began their story. But people say these things because it is the way they relate to the situation. Much of the time they are trying to be empathetic, trying to reach out the best way they can.

Some believe grief is a private matter and do not want to intrude in such delicate matters, so, they give space and hold on to the notion that if someone needs to talk that they will certainly call them. However, that can be difficult. I know it was for me.

We tend to put expectations on others to help us or to meet our needs—many times without discussing it with them. We may think they are letting us down and wonder why they didn't do such and such, or why they did this or that. We cannot put expectations on others which they are unable to fulfill, especially if they do not even know about them.

If we need help from someone, we need to be humble and ask for it, clearly stating what we need and when. Much of the time, others would be more than happy to do anything to help. They also need to respond whether or not they can do what is requested. However, when we really don't know exactly what we need, share that with them, too. Asking someone to, "Maybe give me a call sometime." is different than saying, "I need you to call me today!"

The truth of the matter is that life does go on. Everyone has his or her own situations to deal with. Our society is a very busy one. Between people's jobs, family and routines, there is often very little time for other things.

Tips for Helping Another
Who Is Grieving

WHEN SOMEONE is grieving and is in emotional pain, it is often hard to know what to do to help. Here are some tips gleaned from my perspective while grieving.

Communication is how we connect with each other. People will make the comment that they don't know what to say. They want to say the right thing but might be worried about making things worse. However, just knowing that someone is thinking of us is very helpful.

When we communicate in person, about 90% of the message is conveyed in body language. A smile, a hug, and even tears express our love and concern. Be approachable. Face the person who is grieving and make eye contact. That will show that you care. Even if you don't or can't say anything, the person will remember that you cared and were there for them.

Your tone of voice is also as important a part of communication as your actual spoken words. You may say the same thing, but have it perceived differently by the hearer if said in different tones. Using tender, caring tones will convey your message with love and concern. In the end, the actual words spoken are a small part of communication. I hope that provides you some understanding and relief.

When you do have a conversation with someone who

has experienced loss, actively listen. This means you need to listen more than talk. As the saying goes, there is a reason we have two ears and one mouth. Don't have your own pre-planned agenda for the conversation. Let it go wherever it does. Keep in mind this is about and for the person you wish to support and console, not you. Ask questions that will help make it easier for them to share, such as, "Tell me about a hard decision that you are dealing with right now." Discussing it might reveal something you can help them with. However, before you share something with them, ask yourself how it will benefit them.

Use their loved one's name. Don't be afraid to talk about that person and ask questions about them. Ask what their loved one liked to do, ask about their favorite trip, and so forth. Such discussions will help to keep their memories alive.

When someone who is grieving comes to mind, take that as a prompt from the Lord. Give that person a call or send them a card or message. Don't put it off. Do it right when the thought comes. Time can slip by. A month later when you see them you might say, "I was thinking of you," but that doesn't mean as much as if you had carried through to contact them. If someone said that to me, I might think if it weren't for this face to face contact, I never would have known. Maybe they really needed to talk when your thought of them came to mind. Maybe God was giving you a nudge.

Ask if they would like to meet for coffee or a bite to eat. Just getting them out of the house to somewhere new can be helpful. They may be wanting to get together but not want to bother you. Take the first step by trying to arrange a get-together.

Finally, pray for them. The Holy Spirit might impress you with a Bible verse or passage or song for them. Share it! The person may feel like they are drowning. You can be the one to throw out that lifeline! You may never know what an incredible gift you have given because you listened and reached out.

Eliason Ryan Cooper's Photobook

Eliason Ryan Cooper

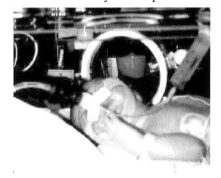

Home at Ten Days Old

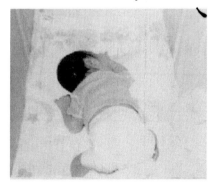

Grandma Faye Moe

Grandma, Great Grandma
Olson, and Mom

Grandma Hug

Pool Time

Picking Blackberries

Grandpa Harlan Moe

Sled Time

Como Zoo

Fishing at Uncle Bob Olson's

Black & White

Golfing with Grandpa

My Favorite Things

My 2nd Birthday

Santa!

Are you OK?

Buddies

My First Trike

My First Bike

Tigger

New Kitties, Oscar & Felix

My First Fish

A Boy and His Fish

The Un-Birthday

My Aunt and Uncles (my Mom's siblings)

Uncle Davey Moe   Auntie Michelle Samuelson

Uncle Mitch Moe   Great Auntie Marian Hedlund

Me with My Cousins

"Dr." Andrew Theis   Feeding Dillon Theis

Kyle & Weston Moe

Kyle & Weston

Dillon & Cameron Theis

Andrew, Weston, Kyle, Cameron, Dillon

Dillon, Kyle, me, Cameron, Weston and Andrew
(photo courtesy of terrygdesen.com)

Last Picture with my cousins

These pictures were taken at my Aunt Michelle's place in Absaraka, ND. (photos courtesy of David Moe)

The Moe Family

Uncle Norman Moe, cousin
Wally Moe, and Grandpa

Aunt May Fulton, Uncle Bob
Moe and wife Aunt Gladys
Moe, Aunt Gen Doland

Uncle Bob Moe's farm

Dancing with Aunt Gen

Moe Reunion Carthage, SD 1998

Little Brother Ryan

Big Brother Dan

Northside Christian School and Church Upon the Rock

Northside CS Basketball Team

Mexico Trip-Ryan B, Aaron, me and Caleb

CUTR Musical Productions

Jake   Ben

Danielle

Youth Conference

Pastor Jean Lund

Mr. Ed

Camp Dinner Activity

Jessie

Jon Riley

Three Amigos – Jon, Ryan B and me at my wedding
(Photo courtesy of Jessica Hegland)

Jon Riley

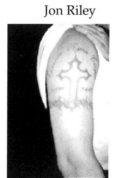

Mom and Jon's Wedding
Photos courtesy of Jessica Hegland)

Remembering Ryan Night
Jake, Caleb, Jon, and Andrew

From Kindergarten to High School

Class of 1998

(photo courtesy of Bill Devlin)

Noah

(photos courtesy of Jessica Hegland)

Helpful Resources

Support Group

GriefShare: a grief recovery support group where you can find help and healing for the hurt of losing a loved one. Groups meet weekly for about nine weeks to help you face these challenges and move toward rebuilding your life.

Books

Grant, Julane. *When Your Friend's Child Dies; A Guide to Being a Thoughtful and Caring Friend*. Portland, Oregon: Angel Hugs Publishing, 1998.

Lewis, C.S. *A Grief Observed*. New York: HarperCollins Publishers, 2001.

Neeld, Ph.D., Elizabeth Harper. *Seven Choices; Taking the steps to new life after loss shatters your world*. Austin, Texas: Centerpoint Press (Third Edition, Revised) a division of MBI Publishing, 1997.

Wolterstorff, Nicholas. *Lament For A Son*. Grand Rapids, MI: Wm. B. Eerdmans Publishing Co, 1987.

Acknowledgments

First, I want to thank God for entrusting me with Ryan, and his loss. He entrusted me with a deep, complicated grief and comforted me throughout this journey. Then, He led me to share my story with others, to pass along this comfort. May He be glorified.

Next, I would like to thank my husband, Jon Straight, for helping me by listening to my thoughts and ideas, supporting me through my frustrations and gamut of emotions while writing this book. You took on many of the household chores which I normally do so I could spend hours and days at the computer.

To my wonderful Church Upon the Rock friends Cheryl Barr, Judy Comstock, and JoAn Brown for reading, and re-reading, my manuscript, offering up your advice and suggestions. The time you devoted to this book is priceless to me. I was at a standstill, not knowing how to take my story to a reader's level. You paved the way! Also, thank you Cheryl for formatting my manuscript for publication and for painting the beautiful front cover picture.

I also want to thank my brother-in-law, Wayne Samuelson, PhD, Family Psychologist, for wanting to be a part of this process. I appreciate your insight and suggestions.

Thank you, Delores Topliff, for editing and polishing my manuscript. You said I should be proud of the finished work, and I am!

And to my good friend, Jessica Hegland, for your enthusiastic support and blessing me with a professional headshot for the back cover!

It is my prayer that this story and God's love will touch and bring healing to those whose hearts have been broken by grief. Without your help this book would not have been written and hurting hearts might not be reached.